Hindu Narratives on Human Rights

Hindu Narratives on Human Rights

Arvind Sharma

Praeger

An Imprint of ABC-CLIO, LLC

ABC-CLIO

Santa Barbara, California • Denver, Colorado • Oxford, England

Library of Congress Cataloging-in-Publication Data

Sharma, Arvind.
Hindu narratives on human rights / Arvind Sharma.
p. cm.
Includes bibliographical references and index.
ISBN 978-0-313-38161-4 (alk. paper) -- ISBN 978-0-313-38162-1 (ebook : alk. paper) 1. Human rights--Religious aspects--Hinduism. 2. Hinduism--Doctrines. I. Title.
BL1215.H84S52 2009
294.5'1723--dc22 2009041629

ISBN 978 0 313 38161 4: paper
ISBN 978 0 313 38162-1: ebook

14 13 12 11 10 1 2 3 4 5

This book is also available on the World Wide Web as an eBook.
Visit www.abc-clio.com for details.

Praeger
An Imprint of ABC-CLIO, LLC

ABC-CLIO, LLC
130 Cremona Drive, P.O. Box 1911
Santa Barbara, California 93116-1911

This book is printed on acid-free paper ♾
Manufactured in the United States of America

Contents

Introduction

Human rights discourse is fast emerging as the global idiom of moral discourse.[1] The process started with the adoption of the Universal Declaration of Human Rights by the United Nations Assembly on December 10, 1948.[2] As work on the text progressed, the word "universal" was substituted for the word "international."[3] It appears doubtful that, had the declaration been called the International Declaration of Human Rights rather than the Universal Declaration of Human Rights, it would have come to possess the moral status it enjoys. The word "international" is so political that it would, in all probability, have led people to view it as a political rather than a moral statement. The substitution of the word "universal" for "international" signaled the desire of its framers to produce a document that reflected not merely a political but a moral consensus. It is part and parcel of the Kantian legacy to the modern world, that the truly moral must be universalizable and, therefore, ultimately universal.[4]

It could be argued that while, one the one hand, the adoption of a "universal" declaration made it less problematic as a document in the moral sense, on the other it makes it more problematic in the context of Hinduism in a religious sense, as Hinduism is often perceived as lacking such a universalistic element, on account of the allegedly particularistic nature of its morality. Such an assumption is widely shared in Western Indology[5] and has also affected not only the understanding of Hinduism in the West, but even Hindu self-understanding to a certain extent as well. Although the view is, in this sense, widespread, it is not, on that account, necessarily correct, as the work of such modern Indian scholars as P. V. Kane has clearly demonstrated.[6] The truth of the matter seems to be that Hinduism pays elaborate and detailed consideration to *both* the particular and the universal dimension of ethics. What seems to have happened is that the particularistic dimension stood out in the perspective of outside observers, to such an extent as to have had the unfortunate effect of obscuring the universal element. The more balanced view is now being increasingly advocated, and perhaps a book such as this will also help tilt the scale in the right direction.

The real difficulty in engaging Hinduism, in the context of human rights, arguably lies not in the *fact* of such moral discourse being present or absent within Hinduism, but in the *manner* in which it is conducted. The way the two words, *morality* and *ethics*, are employed in present-day discussions may help highlight this point. It has been pointed out that

> there is a tendency to use the terms "morality" and "ethics" interchangeably, but when used more precisely, they are not, in fact, interchangeable terms. While morality is a set of norms about what is right and wrong, good and bad, ethics is *reasoning* about morality. We do ethics when we want to determine what is right and wrong so as to guide our behaviour accordingly.[7]

My purpose in citing these lines is not so much to address the issue of how, if at all, morality and ethics may be distinguished, as to alert the reader to the possibility that such *reasoning* could be carried out either privately or publicly. It could, of course, possess both these dimensions, but it is the distinction between the two that must hold our interest at the moment. Readers familiar with the discussion of *anumāna* (inference) in the Nyāya school of Hindu philosophy will be reminded here of the distinction between inference "intended for the sake of others (*parārthānumāna*)," which takes the form of a full-fledged syllogism, ultimately establishing that "Socrates is mortal," and an "inference which is for oneself (*svārthānumāna*) [and] not a formal syllogism; it takes place in the mind of the individual and is not expressed in any verbal form."[8]

In the case of an individual contemplating a course of action, we will find that Hindu ethical reasoning possesses a twofold character: it is both analytical and narrative. The literature of the philosophical schools of India associated with Hinduism, Buddhism, and Jainism focuses primarily on the analytical, whereas the literature associated with a wider audience, such as the one associated with the Epics and the *Purāṇas* focuses on the latter. It is also an interesting feature of Hinduism that, just as particularistic ethics receives much greater attention within it as compared to, say, Christianity, without the universalistic dimension being ignored, *narratives* regarding ethical decision making receive much more space within it, in the course of its engagement with moral and ethical issues, than might be the case with other traditions.

To cut to the chase: when a Hindu is morally perplexed and wants to decide what to do, the Hindu tradition is as likely to offer that person a narrative of how someone acted in a similar situation in the past, with what consequences, as a prescription on how to act. And as most Hindus are not philosophers, despite what people may have come to believe, the decision maker is more likely to find a narrative bearing on the situation, rather than a formal syllogistic analysis, at one's disposal to serve as a catalyst for moral decision making. Although the narrative usually sets an example, this might not always be the case; the narrative could also act as a warning. But narrative it is. The following words of Bimal Krishna Matilal bear citing on this point:

> People tell stories, and they love to hear them. Story-telling is a pervasive feature of all civilizations. Stories are told mainly for entertainment, or at least that is how we regard the activity of story-telling. They are meant to entertain others. However, pure entertainment cannot be the sole purpose of creating and re-creating stories, myths, and various other narrative compositions. Stories must have a meaning. In fact, they must have morals, and morals are connected with the domain of morality and ethics. In this sense, there is a very intimate and inherent connection between story-telling and ethical discourse. We may say that since ethical principles are utterly abstract, and the human tendency toward ethical behaviour (presumably in any civilized society) is very nebulous and sometimes unconscious, ethical discourse receives a local habitation and a name through stories and myths. The story-telling activity has thus one important aspect. It is an unconscious concretization of an abstract moral discourse.[9]

All this, then, is by way of preparing the reader for the situation that Hindu thinking about human rights may be as much available in narrative as in analytical form: hence the description of this book as *Hindu Narratives on Human Rights*, for it focuses on the former.[10]

Chapter I

Right to Justice

The first selection addresses the question of justice, because its theme consists of a demand that justice be done by the king to a widow whose husband has died in shadowy circumstances. A wrong has occurred and it needs to be righted.

The reader might wonder at this point what this quest for justice has to do with the issue of human rights, except in the most general way. This question provides a useful point of entry into the current state of human rights discourse, both in its practical and theoretical dimensions.

I begin by addressing the practical dimension. Both activists and scholars, working in the field of human rights, have long observed a curious phenomenon when a debate on human rights issues is in progress. When this debate is pursued at the theoretical level and directed to such questions as "What are the bases of human rights?" or "Do different cultures have different concepts of human rights?" the debate becomes highly contentious and even fractious. However, once attention is directed to actual cases where human rights have been compromised—as when someone has been imprisoned without a trial or has been tortured by either a government or by terrorists—a consensus that a particular concrete case represents a violation of human rights emerges rapidly within the same group. In other words, whereas the issue of what is a *right* and why it should be considered a right might be a matter of endless debate, the identification of a particular case as representing a *wrong*—as a violation of a right—is often a fairly forthright matter. Justice then consists in the righting of such a wrong. This is one pragmatic reason why human rights discourse can never swerve too far from the tracks of justice.

The connection between human rights and the quest for justice—which involves the righting of a wrong—also plays an important role in the theory of human rights. Human rights discourse has been characterized by a vigorous debate regarding the roots of human rights. Some have argued that human rights are the logical consequence of the doctrine of natural rights, as found in the West; others have argued for their origins in law—that human rights are conferred on us by law. This is sometimes called the positivistic theory of human rights, as distinguished from a natural rights theory of human rights. Still others have located human rights in various theological or philosophical concepts.

It could, however, be argued that it might be possible to root the doctrine of human rights in a doctrine of human wrongs, or what might be called a "deprivation theory of human rights," namely, that human rights come to be identified in the process of their denial or deprivation, just as a treatment is identified in the face of an illness. One scholar who has argued strongly for such a doctrine of human rights, which derives them from human wrongs, is Alan Dershowitz, whose views in the matter deserve to be cited at some length. He expounds this position as follows:

> Building a system of rights from the bottom up, based on the experiences of injustice, is consistent with the common-law approach to the development of legal doctrines. Injustice provides the occasion for change. The history of the common law has been a history of adapting legal doctrine to avoid or minimize injustice. When all parties to a dispute believe that justice has been done, there is no occasion for litigation, no need for dispute resolution, and hence no stimulus to change the law. The case reports are not about instances of perceived justice, but about injustices in search of remedies. Even Aristotle's theory of corrective justice recognized the close relationship between wrongs and the need for corrective law as to restore equilibrium.
>
> The same is true of the history of rights. Where the majority does justice to the minority, there is little need for rights. But where injustice prevails, rights become essential. Wrongs provoke rights, as our checkered history confirms.[1]

In the narrative which follows, it is the wrongful death of the husband that generates the right for the widow to demand justice at the hands of the king.

Most would be inclined to agree that the right to justice is a fundamental human right, although the point is not usually expressed in this way. That is to say, everybody possesses the universal human right to justice, if wronged. This fact stands out boldly in the following narrative, which otherwise contains features that might appear quaint to a modern mind.

The narrative is drawn from the *Rājataraṅgiṇī* and deals with the reign of King Candrāpīḍa (c. 720 CE).

Once a Brahmin woman, who had undertaken a hunger strike, spoke as follows to the king, who was seated in the assembly, upon being questioned by his legal officers.

"You are known as the remover of evil but my husband has been deprived of his life, while peacefully asleep, by an unknown person under your rule.

The premature death of a subject is a matter of grave humiliation for a virtuous king.

Even if under the influence of the wicked age we live in, someone even like you may not take note of it, but how can you be indifferent to this particular crime, which is worse than sin.

Think as I may, I cannot think of anyone who could be my husband's enemy. All the various quarters were cool like white sandal paste for my harmless husband.

He was free from envy and arrogance, soft-spoken, devoted to virtue, and approachable. He was without greed and no one hated him.

There is a Brahmin of the same age as his whom he outshone academically, since childhood. He lives in Mākṣikasvāmin and is well versed in sorcery. He should be considered a suspect.

People who themselves lose out to others in the quest for fame, and spend sleepless nights brooding over their lack of ability, injure those more gifted than them out of jealousy."

■ ■ ■ ■

After the Brahmin woman had thus spoken, the king sent for the Brahmin who was the object of suspicion and asked for an explanation.

The Brahmin woman again said to him: "Majesty! As he is reputed for his knowledge of black magic, he will unscrupulously interfere with the divine test (or ordeal)."

Thereupon the king said to her with a wan face: "If his guilt cannot be established, what can we, who are supposed to be judges, do in the matter?

Even in the case of an ordinary person, no one can be punished if guilt has not been established, then how can a Brahmin be punished, who, even if guilty, is exempt from the death penalty?"[2]

When the king had stopped speaking, the Brahmin's wife spoke again: "Four nights have elapsed since I stopped eating, O king.

I did not commit Satī out of my yearning for revenge against the murderer and I am going to fast to death unless justice is done."

The king himself began observing a solemn fast at the feet of Tribhuvanasvāmī, when he saw the stand taken by the Brahmin woman.

After three nights, Viṣṇu, the best of gods, who is ever awake, spoke these true words to the king, as the night waned:

"O king! This procedure will not work in Kaliyuga; no one can make the sun rise at midnight.

However, an exception is being made on account of the severity of your austerity. Have rice-powder strewn in the courtyard of my temple.

If the print of his footsteps, when he [the suspect] circumambulates the place thrice, is trailed (visibly) by the (ogress) Brahmahatyā, then he deserves to be punished as the culprit. This procedure should be carried out at night, for the sun removes evil during the day."

The procedure was carried out and the Brahmin was found guilty. As the upholder of law, the king awarded him due punishment, which excluded death.

When the king, who was like the (divine) ruler Indra on earth, had sentenced her husband's murderer, the wife of the Brahmin blessed him as follows:

"Many rulers have been born on this earth but only in two cases have even secret crimes been punished—under Kṛtavīrya's son [Sahasrārjuna] and under you, O king.

When you protect the land and chastise the wicked as you rule the country, love and enmity are both realized in their highest measure."

His reign, also very brief, was full of such legal decisions and Solomonic subtleties, worthy of Kṛta Yuga.

Rājataraṅgiṇī IV.82-89 and 93-109

One might object that there is no right to justice as such enunciated in human rights discourse. However, one needs to be careful with an objection such as this. During the Senate hearings of Judge John G. Roberts Jr., a few years ago, when he was asked by a senator at one point "whether he believed that the 'right to privacy' existed in the [American] Constitution, Mr. Roberts replied, 'Senator, I do.'"[3]

A commentator noted that "if he had not, Judge Roberts would have sunk his chances to become the 17th chief justice of the United States just 20 minutes into his 20 hours of confirmation testimony. So many Americans—and so many senators—now accept the concept as an organizing principle of modern life and law that Robert H. Bork's confirmation as an associate justice collapsed 18 years ago this month in the face of his refusal to find such a right."[4]

Now comes the irony: the phrase appears nowhere in the U.S. Constitution. As Todd S. Purdum elaborates:

> But the phrase appears nowhere in the Constitution itself: Privacy to do just what, and with whom, under what circumstances, with the benefit of what technology? There's the rub.[5]

Some rights pervade a whole set of other rights implicitly, even if they have not been enunciated propositionally like these other rights. From a Hindu perspective, this right to justice at the hands of the ruler is one such right, firmly anchored in the Hindu ethos.

The Tamil epic *Śilappadigāram* graphically demonstrates the dire consequences of the abridgement of this right, by way of contrast with the happy outcome when the right is upheld, as illustrated by the account from the *Rājataraṅgiṇī*. The storyline of that epic unfolds as follows. Kovalan and Kaṇṇagi are happily married members of the merchant class, until one day Kovalan meets a danseuse at a festival at the royal court, whose name is Mādavi, and falls in love with her. The love, in running its course, impoverishes Kovalan to the point that he ultimately returns penitently to his wife. They decide to leave the city of Kāvirippaṭṭinam, for that is where they lived, and move to the city of Madurai to make a fresh start, with the "jeweled anklets" of Kaṇṇagi (after which the epic is named) as their sole financial asset.

It so happens that the Queen of the Pandyan king, who ruled over Madurai, had had a similar anklet stolen by her wicked jeweler. The jeweler, on seeing Kovalan in possession of Kaṇṇagi's anklet, identified it as the missing one, whereupon Kovalan was seized and executed as a thief in a major miscarriage of justice. Kaṇṇagi, however, appeared before the king with her remaining anklet, thereby establishing Kovalan's innocence. The king fell to the ground from shock, and Kaṇṇagi, in a terrifying scene, tore apart the left breast of her body with her own hand and was on the point of reducing the city to ashes with her curse, when the patron goddess of the city interceded to prevent such a devastating denouement.

The story also has another implication: that *many* may come to suffer on account of the violation of the right of *one*. That *many may suffer on account of one* is a staple of Indian folklore, as suggested by the following episode from the life of Guru Nānak (1469–1539).

BĀBĀ NĀNAK EXPLAINS THE DESTRUCTION OF SAIDPUR

One day Mardānā asked, "Why have so many been slain when only one did wrong?"

"Go and sleep under that tree, Mardānā," answered the Gurū. "When you get up I shall give you an answer."

And so Mardānā went and slept there. Now a drop of grease had fallen on his chest while he was eating, and while he was sleeping it attracted ants. One ant happened to disturb the sleeping Mardānā, who responded by wiping them all away with his hand.

"What have you done, Mardānā?" asked Bābā Nānak.

"All have died because one disturbed me," exclaimed Mardānā.

Bābā Nānak laughed and said, "Mardānā, thus does death come to many because of one."[6]

The view that the violation of the right of an individual may have consequences, which extend beyond the individual, remains relatively unexplored in classical Western human rights discourse on account of its individualistic orientation, but it was recognised early in Hindu thought. In the case from the *Rājataraṅgiṇī*, the Brahmin's widow had put her life on the line in the quest for justice for the husband, and we don't know how the dominoes would have fallen. In the case of Kaṇṇagi, the failed quest for justice for the husband temporarily imperiled the city.

It is also remarkable that, in both these instances, it is the women who sought to right the wrong done against their husband. A more conservative interpretation would portray them as loyal wives rather than fighters for human rights, but it is difficult to avoid the implication that they were asserting the right to justice.

Chapter 2

Does Hinduism Possess a Concept of Rights?

It is a commonly held view in Western circles that Asia in general, and India in particular, possessed a concept of duty, but not of rights, and that the concept of human rights is of Western origin—even of recent Western origin. Isaiah Berlin writes, for instance:

> The notion of human rights was absent from the legal conceptions of the Romans and the Greeks; this seems to hold equally of the Jewish, Chinese and all other ancient civilizations that have since come to light. The domination of this ideal has been the exception rather than the rule, even in the recent history of the West.[1]

The same view is expressed more forcefully, in an East-West context, by John Donnelly as follows:

> Most non-Western cultural and political traditions lack not only the practice of human rights but also the very concept. As a matter of historical fact, the concept of human rights is an artifact of modern Western civilization.[2]

In the narrative soon to be discussed, however, the focus rests more on the existence of the concept of a right itself, as distinguished from a human right, in Hindu lore, although I have argued elsewhere that even the idea of a human right, especially in its political and civic shade of meaning, may also be identified in ancient Hindu literature.[3] At the moment I am more focused on developing the following point, articulated by Professor J. B. Carman:

> It is worth noting that our Western notion of rights goes back much further than the affirmation of equal rights. What is one's right is what is one's due, whether because of who one is by birth or because of what one has accomplished. It is one's fair share even if it is not an equal share. That notion of right is certainly deeply embedded in the Hindu social system. In the traditional village economy in which very little money changed hands, different laborers and artisans received a prescribed amount or share of the harvest. Their share or "rights" were usually unequal, but they were supposed to be appropriate. The basic right was not a matter of community decision; it was an expression of the particular nature of one's *dharma* as the producer of particular goods (for example, the potter) or the performer of particular services (for example, the washerman).[4]

The point is important because it runs counter to such claims as the following, that "among Eastern philosophers, *rights* have never been a primary category. The Buddhist scholar Hajime Nakamura spoke for most Asian philosophers when he commented: "We don't usually speak of rights in our traditions."[5]

Associated with this position is the complementary view that, at least in such cultures as the Hindu, one speaks not of rights but of duties or that at least one speaks of duties first. This view has the support of no less a person than Mahatma Gandhi.

When asked what he thought of the proposed Universal Declaration of Human Rights, Mahatma Gandhi replied:

> I learnt from my illiterate but wise mother that all rights to be deserved and preserved came from duty well done. Thus, the very right to live accrues to us only when we do the duty of citizenship of the world. From this one fundamental statement, perhaps it is easy enough to define the duties of Man and of Woman and correlate every right to some corresponding duty to be first performed.[6]

The point to note is that the concept of right did exist, and, although it was often correlated to duty, this was not always the case, as becomes apparent at the end of the narrative that follows.

Hence, in embarking on a study of human rights in Hinduism as such, it might be worthwhile to begin with a more fundamental query: Does Hinduism possess a concept of *rights* per se, prior to discussing whether it possesses a concept of *human rights*?

A well-known, even notorious, incident in the *Mahābhārata* bears on this point. A game of dice is in progress at the Kuru court. It is being played between the Kauravas on the one hand and the Pāṇḍavas on the other. These two parties constitute the main antagonists in the epic, who are descended from common ancestors but now find themselves embroiled in a dynastic dispute involving succession to the throne, which is temporarily occupied by Dhṛtarāṣṭra, the father of the hundred sons who collectively constitute the Kauravas. His brother, now dead, had five sons through his two wives, who are collectively known as the Pāṇḍavas. Their names are Yudhiṣṭhira, Bhīma, Arjuna, Nakula, and Sahadeva, and they are all married to the same wife—Draupadī. In a bid to avert fraternal strife over the throne, Dhṛtarāṣṭra divides the kingdom between them and his hundred sons (led by Duryodhana). The part of the kingdom allotted to the Pāṇḍavas, with its capital at Indraprastha, soon begins to prosper to the point that they choose to perform the Vedic royal sacrifice called *rājasūya.* Their jealous rivals, the Kauravas, feel frustrated by the rise of the Pāṇḍavas, who, however, are too strong for them to be defeated in battle. Nor can they rely on their own allies, some of whom had begun sending tribute to the Pāṇḍavas. Duryodhana's maternal uncle, Śakuni, proposes a dice match, for he is good at it and loves to play it, whereas Yudhiṣṭhira loves it but is not good at it. Although some of his advisers are against it, Dhṛtarāṣṭra overrules them out of his love for his son, which is depicted in the epic as his fatal weakness. The stage is thus set. Yudhiṣṭhira plays on behalf of the Pāṇḍavas, and Śakuni on behalf of the Kauravas. Yudhiṣṭhira soon hits a losing streak, brought about by trickery according to the account, and is on the point of running out of chips. Śakuni says: "You have lost great wealth, you have lost your brothers, your horses and elephants. Now tell me . . . if you have anything left to stake."[7]

At this point, Yudhiṣṭhira stakes himself and loses and is then egged on by Śakuni to stake Draupadī, the wife in common of all the Pāṇḍavas. He does so and loses again.

At this point Duryodhana, the leader of the Kauravas, asks the steward to go and fetch Draupadī, the spoils of victory.

We plug into the narrative at this point. The narrator is Vaiśampāyana.

Vaiśampāyana said:	The son of Dhṛtarāstra, mad with pride saying, "Fie on you, steward," saw the usher in the assembly and said to him in the middle of the elders: "You, usher, go and get Draupadī. You need not fear the Pāṇḍavas. This timid steward disputes the point but then he never did wish us well."

Thus spoken to, the usher, a bard, left quickly on hearing the words of the king and approached the queen of the Pāṇḍavas, entering like a dog in a lion's den.

The usher said: O Draupadī! You have been won by Duryodhana from Yudhiṣṭhira in his crazy addiction to gambling. Go to the house of Dhṛtarāṣṭra. O Draupadī, I will guide you to your chores.

Draupadī said: How dare you talk like that to me, usher! Which prince will gamble with his wife? The king has lost his mind in his addiction to gambling. Was there nothing else left to stake?

The usher said: When there was nothing else left to stake, Yudhiṣṭhira staked you. He had already lost his brothers and himself; then O princess, he lost you.

Draupadī said: O son of a bard, go to the game and ask in the assembly: "Whom did you lose first, yourself or me?"

Return after finding this out and then come to fetch me, O son of a bard.

Vaiśampāyana said: He then went to the assembly and repeated the words of Draupadī: "As whose owner did you lose me?" Draupadī asks of you. "Whom did you lose first, yourself, or was it me?" Yudhiṣṭhira, however, seemed lost and lifeless. He did not say anything either way to the bard by way of reply.

Duryodhana said: Let Draupadī come here and ask the question. Let everyone here hear her words and his.

Vaiśampāyana said: The subordinate of Duryodhana went to the palace, and that usher and bard said to Draupadī painfully:

O Princess, the delegates summon you. It seems to me the fall of Kauravas is on hand. That low person will not maintain good grace if, O Princess, you go to the assembly.

Draupadī said: This is what has been ordained by the ordainer. Laying his hand on both the wise man and the fool, he said: "*Dharma* is supreme in the world." He will take care of our well-being, if we protect it.

Vaiśampāyana said: On hearing what Duryodhana wanted to do, Yudhiṣṭhira sent a messenger acceptable to Draupadī, O best of Bharatas.

Draupadī came and stood in front of the father-in-law with one garment, which was knotted low down, and weeping, at a time when she was having her period.

Then seeing the face of those courtiers, king Duryodhana said to the messenger with glee: "O usher, bring her right here so that she may be able to speak to Kauravas facing them."

Then the usher, his subordinate, who was afraid of Draupadī's wrath, let go of his pride and said again to the assembled, "Who am I to say anything to Draupadī?"

Duryodhana said: "O Duḥśāsana, this bard's son is terrified of Bhīma, this fool. Go yourself and grab and bring her. Your rivals are helpless." Then that son of a king rose, on hearing the words of his brother, his eyes redshot with anger. He entered the place of the mighty warriors and spoke to Draupadī, the daughter of kings, as follows:

"O Draupadī, come, come. You are won. Put bashfulness aside and look at Duryodhana. Your eyes are like large lotuses. Please the Kurus. We have gained you lawfully. Enter the hall."

Then rising, she wiped her listless face and, with a deeply troubled mind, desperately ran to where the women of the old king Dhṛtarāṣṭra were.

Then Duḥśāsana rushed in roaring rage and grabbed the queen by her long flowing dark hair.

The hair, which had been anointed with water after being purified with holy spells at the concluding bath of the Rājasūya sacrifice, were now outrageously stroked by the son of Dhṛtarāṣṭra, robbing the Pāṇḍavas of their valour.

He stroked her and brought Draupadī to the hall, her hair dark of the deepest dye, and tossed her, desperate, in the presence of her husbands, as if she had none, as a wind tosses a plaintain tree.

As she was being dragged, she said softly, her body bent: "This is my time of the month. You fool, I am wearing a single garment. I cannot be taken into the hall like this, you cad."

Then he said to her, holding Draupadī tightly by the dark tresses:

"Call for help to Kṛṣṇa or Jiṣṇu, and Hari and Nara. I am carrying you off.

O Draupadī, you may be in your periods or with one piece of cloth or without any whatever. You have been won at stake and have been made into a slave-woman. One has sex with slave women as one likes."

Her hair disheveled, her garment half gone, and all shaken-up by Duḥśāsana, ashamed and burning with fury, Draupadī whispered and said:

"I cannot stand like this in this assembly in front of these elders or those who are as esteemable as elders, who are learned in the scriptures, who perform the rites, and who are all like Indra.

You cruel cad, stop stripping me, stop dragging me. The princes will not forgive you this, even if the gods, along with Indra, come to your help.

The king is the son of *Dharma* and established in *dharma*. *Dharma* is hard to know, even by an expert. But I am not willing to commit even an iota of a misdeed and give up my virtue at the behest of my husband.

This is indeed an ignoble deed you commit, dragging me while I am in my period amid the Kaurava heroes. No one will respect you for this, although they don't mind what you are doing.

The chivalrous code of honor of the Bharatas is lost indeed, and the warrior's honor[8] too is gone, now that the Kauravas merely watch sitting in the hall as the bounds of propriety among the Kurus are transgressed.

Droṇa and Bhīṣma are not men of substance, nor surely this high-souled person, as the main elders of the Kuru clan take no note as this king commits such an egregious breach of decorum."

Thus wailing, the slim Draupadī cast a scornful glance at her seething husbands, the Pāṇḍavas, inflaming them, whose bodies were bursting with indignation at her sidelong glances.

The pain felt at the loss of kingdom, or wealth, or of precious jewels was nothing compared to the pain inflicted by the furious sidelong glances of the desperate Draupadī.

And Duḥśāsana watched Draupadī as she looked at those miserable husbands and then, shaking her wildly, who had almost fainted, branded her a "slave-woman," laughing uproariously.

Karṇa was very pleased to hear this and applauded him, laughing loudly. And Subala's son, the king of Gāndhāra, similarly cheered Duḥśāsana on.

Those others who happened to be in the assembly, apart of from these two (Duḥśāsana and Karṇa) and Duryodhana, felt sorely distressed at seeing Draupadī being dragged in the assembly.

Bhīṣma said: "My dear! I am unable to answer your question properly on account of the legal subtlety involved. On the one hand one who does not possess his own wealth cannot stake another's, but on the other one must consider that the wives are the possession of the husband.

Yudhiṣṭhira can give up the entire bountiful earth, but he will not abandon truth. Yudhisthira said 'I have lost.' Therefore I can't solve this puzzle.

Śakuni is second to none in playing dice. And Yudhiṣṭhira was given this option by him. The high-souled Duryodhana does not think it unfair.

Therefore I can't answer your question."

Draupadī said: "The king was called in the assembly by cunning, wicked, ignoble cheats, who love to gamble. [But the king] is not experienced at it. Why was the choice left with him?

He is sincere and did not realize he was being cheated—that he was defeated by others ganging up on him, only then did he stake me.

The Kurus present in this assembly are the proud owners of sons and daughters-in-law. May they all examine my words and answer my question properly."

Vaiśampāyana said: While Draupadī spoke thus, crying piteously and looking at her humiliated husband, Duḥśāsana kept making harsh, unpleasant, and coarse comments.

Bhīma saw her who was been dragged, in her courses, whose garment had slipped away, and who did not deserve all this, and then looked at Yudhiṣṭhira and then gave vent to his anger in extreme anguish.

Mahābhārata II.60

Bhīma said: "O Yudhiṣṭhira, many wenches are found in the country of gamblers, but they do not play dice with them; even they have that much compassion. The tribute obtained from the king of Kāśī and all the other excellent items, as well as the jewels brought by other kings, the vehicles and money and the coats of mail and weapons, the kingdom, you yourself and we as well, have been gambled away to others. I did not take offense at that, for you are the master of all. But I think in staking Draupadī you went too far. She deserves better, having gained the Pāṇḍavas as a girl, she is being harassed by petty and cruel rogues because of you. For her sake, O king, I cast my fury at you. I shall incinerate your arms. Sahadeva! Fetch the fire."

Arjuna said: "O Bhīmasena, never before have such words been uttered by you. Cruel enemies have destroyed your respect for *dharma*. Don't do what others would love to see you do. Follow your highest calling. No one should ever overstep the eldest lawful brother. The king was summoned by others, and, abiding by the code of chivalry, he gambled because others wanted him to. That goes to our great credit."

Bhīmasena said: "O Arjuna, if I thought that Yudhiṣṭhira had staked her for his own aggrandisement, then I would burn both his arms together perforce in blazing fire."

Vaiśampāyana said: Upon seeing the Pāṇḍavas suffering in this way, and Draupadī in torment, Vikarṇa spoke up thus.

"O kings! Reply to what has been said by Draupadī. If we remain indecisive in our response, we go to hell right way. Bhīṣma and Dhṛtarāṣṭra are the seniormost Kuru elders, and they have together spoken not a word, neither has the wise Vidura. Droṇa the teacher of all, as well as Kṛpa, even these two eminent Brahmins have not responded to the question. Those other kings who have assembled here from the four corners of the earth should say something as they deem fit, setting aside partisan feelings. May the kings deliberate on the statement made by auspicious Draupadī and then state who stands where."

In this way he repeatedly addressed the members of the assembly, but the kings did not say anything for or against. Having addressed all the kings again and again in this way, Vikarṇa wrung his hands and said with a sigh:

"The kings may or may not reply to what has been said, but O Kauravas, let me tell you how I think justice is served in this situation. The best of men have identified four vices of kings: hunting, drinking, gambling, and fornicating. One addicted to these stands out as one who has abdicated morality, and people do not consider the actions of an immoral person as valid. Draupadī was staked by Yudhiṣṭhira under the sway of addiction, when he was challenged by tricksters. This blameless Draupadī is the common wife of all the Pāṇḍavas. She was staked by Yudhiṣṭhira, who had gambled his freedom away. She was mentioned by Duḥśāsana when he wanted a stake. After taking all this into account, I don't think she has been won."

Upon hearing this, a huge roar arose from the members of the audience, praising Vikarṇa and denouncing Duḥśāsana. When the noise had subsided, Karṇa, almost faint with anger, grasped his shining arm and spoke as follows:

"There are many distortions in what has been said by Vikarṇa. They will destroy him, just as the fire-stick is consumed by the very fire it generates. Even though urged by Draupadī, these [elders] have said nothing. I believe that they think that Draupadī has been won fair and square. O Vikarṇa, son of Dhṛtarāṣṭra, you will be rent to pieces by your childishness, for you, a child, speak like an elder in the assembly. O younger brother of Duryodhana, you do not know the law correctly when you say that Draupadī has not been won, when she has been. O son of Dhṛtarāṣṭra, how can you say that Draupadī has not been won, when Yudhiṣṭhira staked all that he had in the assembly. O best of Bharatas, Draupadī is included in all that he owns, so how do you hold that Draupadī was not won fairly, when she was. She was mentioned by name and permitted to be staked by the Pāṇḍavas; then for what reason do you say that she was not won? And if you think that she was brought unfairly into this assembly, with only one piece of clothing on, then listen to what I have to say in response. O scion of the Kurus, the gods have ordained one husband for a woman. She is definitely a slut, because she resorts to many. I don't think there is anything strange in bringing her into the assembly, whether draped in one piece of cloth or none. She, as well as the Pāṇḍavas and all their wealth—all these riches have been won by Duḥśāsana, as per law. O Duḥśāsana, this Vikarṇa is just a child mouthing wisdom. Strip the Pāṇḍavas of their clothes and Draupadī's as well."

On hearing this, O descendant of Bharata, all the Pāṇḍavas discarded their upper garments and sat down in the assembly.

Then, O king, Duḥśāsana forcibly grabbed hold of the garment of Draupadī and began to strip her in the middle of the assembly. O king, as the garment was pulled away, another one like it appeared in its place time and again. Then a pandemonium broke loose, as all the kings watched such a miraculous happening occur in the world. Then and there Bhīma, in the midst of kings, cursed in a mighty voice, with his lips trembling with anger, kneading his hands.

"Warriors who dwell on this earth, take my words to heart. Nothing like this has been uttered by anyone before, nor will be. O kings, if I do not live up to them after having uttered them, then may I not find a place among all my ancestors, if I do not drink the blood from the chest of this bastard felon, an outcaste of the Bharatas, after tearing it open in battle." On hearing his words, which thrilled the whole world, they paid him homage and condemned Dhṛtarāṣṭra's son. When the heap of garments got piled up in the middle of the assembly, then Duḥśāsana sat down, exhausted and ashamed. Then the Brahmins in the assembly raised a hair-raising cry of "Fie!" when they saw the sons of Kuntī. And the people shouted, "The Kauravas do not answer the question," deploring Dhṛtarāṣṭra. Then Vidura, who know all about law, raised his hand and, holding off the assembled members, spoke as follows.

Vidura said: "Draupadī has asked a question and is crying like an orphan. The members of the assembly have not answered her question, and justice is being compromised. When an oppressed person comes to an assembly like a blazing fire, then he should be appeased with truth and justice. When in anguish a person raises a question of justice among the members of the assembly, then they should address it without partisan passion and rancor. O kings, Vikarṇa has answered the question according to his own lights, and you should also respond to it as you deem fit. One, who, while present in the hall, and seeing the law, does not answer it, then he gets half of the guilt that accrues from telling a lie. And one who, while present in the hall, and seeing the law, states the facts falsely, doubtless incurs the entire guilt of telling a lie.

On this point an ancient story is cited in the form of a dialogue between Prahlāda and sage Aṅgirasa. Prahlāda was a king of the demons. He had a son called Virocana, who got into a hassle with Sudhanvā, the son of Aṅgirasa, over a girl. Out of desire for the girl, each claimed superiority over the other and staked even their lives over it, it is said. They took their dispute to Prahlāda, asking him: "Tell us who among us is better of the two and do not lie." He looked at Sudhanvā, frightened by this dispute. Sudhanvā got enraged and, blazing like the holy staff, said to him: "If you will tell a lie or not answer the question, then Indra will shatter your head in a hundred pieces with his thunderbolt." Thus spoken to by Sudhanvā, Prahlāda began to tremble like the leaf of the *aśvattha* tree. The demon approached the brilliant sage Kaśyapa to ask him about this.

Prahlāda said: "You know the law as it prevails both among the gods and the demons. O wise one, now listen to a legal problem pertaining to Brahmanic law. If a person does not respond to an issue, or responds to it falsely, then tell me how he fares in the hereafter. I ask you."

Kaśyapa said: "If a person knows the answer but does not answer the question out of passion, anger, or fear, then he makes himself the target of a thousand nooses of Varuṇa. He is liberated from one noose at the end of the year. Therefore one who knows should straightaway tell the truth. When justice pierced by injustice enters a hall and the members of the assembly do not remove the dart, then all of them get pierced by it. The leader takes half, and the doer of the act takes a fourth, and the members of the assembly take a fourth—if they fail to condemn the condemnable. But where what deserves to be censured is censured, then the leader remains sinless, the members of the assembly remain free of it, and the sin accrues to the performer of the deed. O Prahlāda, those who tell a falsehood when asked destroy the fruits of all their pious and charitable deeds for seven generations backward and forward. The lords of the Thirty Gods place the following griefs on par: one whose property has been stolen, one whose son has been killed, one who is in trouble as a debtor, one who is being persecuted by a king, a woman who has become a widow, one who has strayed away from a caravan, one whose husband has taken a second wife, and one who has been let down by witnesses. One who tells a lie invites them all. Witness is said to be one who sees or hears something himself. Therefore a witness does not lose out on *dharma* and *artha* if he tells the truth."

Vidura said: Prahlāda told his son, upon hearing the words of Kaśyapa: "Sudhanvā is better than you, just as Aṅgirasa is better than me. Sudhanvā's mother is better than yours. Virocana, you life is now in the hands of Sudhanvā."

Sudhanvā said: "Since you stand firm in virtue disregarding the love of your son, I set your son free. May he live a hundred years."

Vidura said: "Now that you have heard the ultimate law, let all the members of the assembly ponder what is to be done next in relation to the question raised by Draupadī."

Vaiśampāyana said: The kings said not a word, upon hearing the words of Vidura. Karṇa said to Duḥśāsana: "Take the slave-girl Draupadī to the house." Duḥśāsana dragged away poor Draupadī, trembling and ashamed, and crying out for the Pāṇḍavas.

Mahābhārata II.61

Draupadī said: "Something that I should have done earlier I would like to do now. I was beside myself by being forcibly dragged by a strong man. I would like to acknowledge the elders in the assembly of the Kurus. Let it not be held against me that I did not do this."

Vaiśampāyana said: Shaken violently by him, that poor woman fell down out of despair and cried aloud, as follows in the assembly. She was not used to being treated like this.

Draupadī said: "I, who was seen by the kings on the dais at the time of the Svayaṃvara ceremony and never since, am now present in this assembly. I was not visible even to wind and the sun earlier in my own home, and now I am to be seen in the middle of the assembly of the Kurus. The Pāṇḍavas, who would not bear to see me touched by the wind, put up now with my being touched by this miscreant. I guess times have changed, that even the Kurus permit their bride and daughter to be tormented like this, although she does not deserve it. What can be more humiliating than this, that I, a woman, devout and auspicious, should be plunged in the middle of the assembly. Is nothing left of the *dharma* of kings? I had heard that virtuous women are not led in front of the assembly. That immemorial tradition among the Kauravas has apparently perished. How is it that, being the wife of the Pāṇḍavas, the sister of Dhṛṣtadyumna, and a friend of Kṛṣṇa, I have come to this assembly? Tell this wife of Yudhiṣṭhira, who belongs to the same class as he does, whether she is a slave-girl or not. O Kauravas, I shall act accordingly. This base man, a blot on the name of the Kauravas, molests me severely. O Kauravas, I don't think I can bear this any longer. Whether the kings consider me won or not, I would like to have an answer. I shall act accordingly, O Kauravas."

Bhīṣma said: "O good woman! I have already said that lofty is the path of virtue. Even the high-souled Brahmins cannot discern it in the world. What the powerful person takes to be right in this world, others also say it to be so when the question of what is right comes up. I am unable to reach a conclusive decision in regard to your question on account of its subtlety and profundity and the importance of the matter on hand. The end of this lineage seems to be near, for all the members of the Kuru family are now given to greed and delusion. Those born in high families, good woman, even when assailed by difficulties, do not deviate from the path of justice, just as you stand as our bride. O Draupadī, your conduct entirely becomes you; even when facing difficulties, you still seek virtue. All these elders who know the law, such as Droṇa and others, are present here with empty bodies, drooping and lifeless. I think Yudhiṣṭhira is qualified to answer your question. He can himself say whether you have been won or not."

Vaiśampāyana said: Having seen her in this plight for long, crying like a wounded osprey, the kings did not say anything in favor or against, out of fear of Duryodhana.

Then having glanced at the sons and grandsons of the kings who held their peace, Duryodhana began to smile and spoke to Draupadī as follows. "Let this be a question for your capable husbands—Bhīma, Arjuna, Sahadeva and Nakula, O Draupadī. Let them respond to what you have put forth. Let they say for your sake, Draupadī, that Yudhiṣṭhira is not your master in the midst of these noble people. By falsifying

Yudhiṣṭhira, O Draupadī, they will free you from slavery. The high-souled, virtuous king, like unto Indra and firm in virtue, must himself declare whether he is your lord or not. You must choose one or the other in accordance with what he says. All these Kauravas in the assembly, who share your sorrow—these noble ones—do not speak accordingly, looking at your unfortunate husbands."

Then all the members of the assembly praised the words of Duryodhana in a loud voice. They also danced and waved their clothes. But the cries of "woe" were also heard. All the kings were pleased and applauded the just course of action proposed by Duryodhana. All the kings looked toward Yudhiṣṭhira with their faces turned sideways, wondering what he might say and wondering what Arjuna might say, undefeated in battle, who inspired terror, or Bhīma, or the twins Nakula and Sahdeva. Great was the excitement. Then when the noise had died down, Bhīma spoke as follows, grasping his ample arm, "If our elder, Yudhiṣṭhira, the *dharma* king, had not been our lord, we would not have tolerated this. He owns our merits, as well as our lives. It is because he considers himself defeated that we consider ourselves defeated. No mortal who walks on this earth would have escaped from me alive if he had so much as touched a hair of Draupadī. Look at my arms, round and long like a gate-bolt; even Indra cannot escape once caught in their gridlock. I do not wreak havoc, bound by the noose of *dharma*, constrained by its gravity, and restrained by Arjuna. Once unleashed by Yudhiṣṭhira, I will pulverize these sinful followers of Dhṛtarāṣṭra with the flats of my hand, sharp as swords, as a lion reduces small game to pulp. Then Bhīṣma, Droṇa, and Vidura said: "Bear with us. It is indeed so. With you anything is possible."

Mahābhārata II.62

Karṇa said: "These three cannot own property: a slave, a disciple, and a dependent woman. You, my dear, are now the wife of a slave, his wealth now. You are without masters, and a slave and slave property.

Come in and gratify us with your services, with whatever remains to be done upon entering the house. O princess, now your lords are no longer all those men of Pṛthā (Pāṇdavas), but the men of Dhṛtarāṣṭra.

Quickly choose another husband, young woman, so that your freedom is not gambled away. You should know that a slave moving freely among the masters is not to be reproached.

Nakula, Bhīmasena, Yudhiṣṭhira, Sahadeva, and Arjuna have been defeated (enslaved). O Draupadī, come inside as a slave. They have been defeated and are no longer your husbands.

Of what use to him does Yudhiṣṭhira think are his valor and manliness, now that he has gambled away the daughter of king Drupada of Pāñcāla in the middle of the hall with throws of dice?"

Vaiśampāyana said:	Bhīmsena, upon hearing this, found it unbearable and sighed much in anguish, committed to the king and bound by the noose of law as he was, branding him with his eyes blood-shot with anger.
Bhīma said:	"I am not angry at Karṇa; it is true that the ways of the slaves are upon us. But could my enemies have held me back, if, O king, you had not wagered her?"
Vaiśampāyana said:	Upon hearing the words of Karṇa, King Duryodhana spoke to Yudhiṣṭhira as follows, who sat there silent and senseless: "O king! Bhīma and Arjuna and the twins (Nakula and Sahadeva) take their orders from you. Answer then the question, whether you think that Draupadī has not been won." He said this to Yudhiṣṭhira and then, crazy with power, looked smilingly at Draupadī removing his garment. Smiling connivingly at Karṇa and, as if taunting Bhīma, he exposed his left thigh, while Draupadī was looking on, which bore auspicious marks and was like the trunk of a plaintain tree and an elephant and firm like a thunderbolt. As Bhīma saw this, his red eyes widened, and he delcared in the midst of the kings, announcing it in the assembly, as it were: "May Bhīma be denied the company of his ancestors if he does not smash this thigh with a club in battle." Flames burst forth from all his orifices in anger as from the hollows of a burning tree.
Vidura said:	"Watch out for Bhīma, as for the noose of king Varuṇa. The calamity that the gods had set in motion earlier on the Bharatas has come to pass. The men of Dhṛtarāṣṭra have rolled the dice too far, now that they fight over a woman in an assembly. A great peril endangers their well-being, and the Kurus are plotting evil. This point of law should be quickly resolved, O Kurus. If it is not resolved properly, it will discredit the assembly. If he had staked her earlier in the dice-game, he would have been her owner, because he would not have ceased to be his master. I think a roll by one who has no right on the stake is like a stake won in a dream. Now that

you have heard Duryodhana, speak, O Kurus; do not dodge your duty."

Duryodhana said: "I stand by what Bhīma, Arjuna, and Nakula and Sahadeva say. If they say Yudhiṣṭhira was not their master, I shall set Draupadī free."

Arjuna said: "The *Dharma*-king, high-souled Yudhiṣṭhira, was our master in the earlier throws, but what does he own once he has been enslaved?—that all of you Kurus have to decide."

Vaiśampāyana said: Then in the house of king Dhṛtarāṣṭra, at the time of *agni hotra*, a jackal barked loudly, and, O king, the donkeys brayed back in response, and fierce birds cried out all around.

That terrible sound was heard by the insightful Vidura, as well as by Duḥśāsana. Bhīṣma and Droṇa and the wise Gautama uttered blessings in a loud voice.

Then Gāndhārī and the wise Vidura, upon observing these evil omens, agonizingly apprised the king. Then the king spoke as follows in that assembly of the foremost among the Kurus:

"You, dumb Duryodhana, are done for, now that in the (open) assembly of the foremost among the Kurus you talk like this to a woman, you cad!—and that to a lawfully wedded wife such as Draupadī!"

Having spoken thus, the high-minded Dhṛtarāṣṭra, who had the well-being of his relations at heart, moved away, and now, knowing the facts, he spoke consolingly as follows to Draupadī after considering the matter wisely.

Dhṛtarāṣṭra said: "O Draupadī, choose a boon, ask from me whatever you want. You are most distinguished among my brides—pious and devout."

Draupdī said: "O bull among the Bharatas! Give me this boon, this I choose. May the illustrious Yudhiṣṭhira, who practices every virtue, no longer remain a slave.

Let it not come to pass that the bright Prativindhya (my son through Yudhiṣṭhira), when his mates see him coming, is addressed by them as "Here comes the son of a slave" in their ignorance.

O descendant of Bharata! After having been a prince and being spoiled like no one else ever, he would be destroyed if he were seen to be the son of a slave."

Dhṛtarāṣṭra said: "Good woman, I give you a second boon. Ask of me. My mind tells me that you deserve more than one boon."

Draupadī said: "As my second boon I choose Bhīma and Arjuna and Nakula and Sahadeva, in possession of their chariots and bows."

Dhṛtarāṣṭra said: "Two boons do not do honor to you; choose a third boon from me. Of all my daughters-in-law, you walk best in the way of righteousness."

Draupadī said: Greed destroys virtue, sir. I dare not ask for more. O best of kings, I am not fit to receive a third boon. The *vaiśya*, they say, may ask for one boon; a *kṣatriya* and his wife two; best of kings, a king may ask for three, and a *brāhmaṇa* for a hundred. My husbands have been rescued after having been worsened. They will, O king, obtain good things by their virtuous deeds."

Mahābhārata II.63

The sequence of events previously described imbricates many rights and many perspectives on the history of rights. The question of Draupadī's presence at the assembly provides an interesting wedge here from a historical point of view. If the assembly is treated as a *sabhā*, the question arises: "Who constituted the *sabhā?* The term *sabheya*, applied to *vipra*, indicates that, when it was convened for administrative purposes, it was a gathering of the elect, namely of *brāhmaṇas* and the elders. One late ṚgVedic reference speaks of woman as *sabhāvatī*, worthy of going to the *sabhā*, which shows that woman members attended this body."[9]

Such was the situation in Vedic times, "but subsequently the *sabhā* came to assume a mainly patriarchal and aristocratic character. Woman attended it in the earlier period, but the practice stopped in later Vedic times. In connection with the Draupadī episode, reference is made to the immemorial custom according to which women did not attend the *sabhā*. The very term came to mean a body of men shining together, which suggests that those who sat on it were men of distinction."[10]

The issue of Draupadī's appearance thus provides a window through which we can see how rights have varied over time. In the ṚgVedic times the appearance of women would, in the discourse of human rights, involve the right of public participation, and to *prevent* them from attending the *sabhā* would constitute a violation of the right. By the time of the *Mahābhārata*, the situation has changed so radically as to become the opposite. To *compel* a woman to attend the *sabhā* now constituted a violation of her right to privacy. This example is an object lesson in how a text dealing with human rights must be understood in context.

Apart from pointing to the mutability of rights in the Hindu context, especially given the long and chequered history of Hinduism, the incidents alluded to in the reading also point to the issue of the agency involved in enforcing rights, especially when they are also contested. Two examples serve to illustrate the point. It is clear from the reading selected from the *Mahābhārata* that Yudhiṣṭhira *did* stake his wife, even though whether he had the right to do so remains an open question. The story of Nala and Damyantī within the *Mahābhārata* is said by some to "miniaturize" the *Mahābhārata* story itself, on account of the shared ground between the two. Like Yudhiṣṭhira, Nala gambles away his kingdom, and, after many trials and tribulations involving him and his wife, Damyantī, finally regains it. B. K. Matilal remarks:

> Yudhiṣṭhira was invited to gamble. He accepted the invitation and lost everything. Gambling was a very popular sport of the princes at the time of the *Mahābhārata*. In the story of Nala, the hero lost everything in gambling, but he did not stake his wife, although he was challenged to do so by his opponent. The substory encapsulates the main story and underlines certain points in it. Nala had the good sense to withdraw at the last moment. However, Yudhiṣṭhira went all the way. The bigger the story, the greater the blunder. He staked and lost not only his four brothers, but also his wife Draupadī, who was then dragged into the court and utterly humiliated by the wretched Duḥśāsana. This was probably the worst form of humiliation that Duryodhana succeeded in inflicting upon the Pāṇḍavas. Not only that, it was a sin against humanity, at least from our modern point of view, and he had to pay dearly for it at the end. From this point onward, I believe, it was impossible for the *Mahābhārata* story to end in any other way but with the crushing defeat of Duryodhana.[11]

The point specially worth noting appears early in the passage—that Nala did not stake his wife when challenged to do so, whereas Yudhiṣṭhira did. Now let us assume that ancient Hindu legal practice allowed the husband to gamble away his wife. Who would then have implemented this (inhuman) right, if the husband had insisted on doing so and the wife resisted it? The question is whether the right could only be "privately" implemented, and, if the wife refused, the husband could not do much about it, or whether it could be "publicly" asserted, in the sense that the state machinery could be used to enforce it. This points to a peculiar paradox of human rights discourse—that, although many of these rights are meant to curb the power of the state, many of them rely on the power of the state for their enforcement.

This incident not only points to the mutability and ambiguity in the matter of rights, it also points to their intricacy—in the sense that they might nestle in each other. The question of Draupadī's rights at the assembly and Duroyadhana's right to take her cannot be divorced from Duryodhana's right to claim the throne, such as he might have possessed.

If, for a moment, we look upon the Pāṇḍavas and Kauravas as contestants, and not as heroes and villains, the point is easier to grasp. If we further look upon rights idiom as one way in which we organize our conflicts, the point perhaps becomes even more clear. It is then possible to look upon the dispute between Pāṇḍava and the Kauravas as one of contested rights—a point that becomes clear when the Pāṇḍavas try to negotiate a settlement with the Kauravas in a "land for peace" deal. Ironically, this incident also indicates the poverty of the rights approach, when the two parties have come to view their claims not in terms of rights so much as in terms of right and wrong, with hints of moral absolutism. Then the issue acquires a moral charge that might be too much for rights discourse to handle.

Chapter 3

Freedom of Religion

The role played by the concept of religious freedom, in the context of the emergence of human rights, has often not been fully appreciated, and this might well be the place to begin to rectify the situation. One of the few scholars who has paid careful attention to this point is T. Patrick Burke, and we shall follow his lead to begin with. He emphasizes the connection of religious freedom to the emergence of a liberal society, within which human rights flourish. He writes,

> Across the street from Boston Common, in front of the state House, stands the statue of a Quaker woman, Mary Dyer, who was hanged there in 1660. The only crime she had committed was that of being a Quaker in a Puritan society. Her statue, generously erected by the Puritans' descendants, is a silent testimony to a revolution of thought and feeling which divides what we may call the modern world from everything which preceded it as effectively as the Himalayas divide India from China. She was hanged because to the world of the Middle Ages and for some time afterwards it seemed a self-evident truth that a society could only afford to have one religion.[1]

The acceptance of religious freedom as a basic principle in the formative phase of the United States of America broke from this tradition. As T. Patrick Burke explains,

> At the time of the founding of the United States, however, a historic change took place. Several of the colonies had their own religious traditions: Massachusetts was Puritan and Congregationalist, Pennsylvania was Quaker,

> Virginia and the Carolinas were Anglican. But during the eighteenth century a more tolerant spirit had taken hold, probably under the impact of the Enlightenment, and the colonies had each loosened many of their restrictions on other forms of religion than their own. Furthermore, if they were going to found one nation together, they could scarcely afford to put one another to death for religious differences. The members of the First Congress therefore agreed, and enshrined it in the First Amendment to the Constitution, that the new federal government "shall make no law respecting an establishment of religion, or prohibiting the free exercise thereof. . . ." The United States was to have freedom of religion. The actual implementation of this provision in the sense in which we understand it today took some time. But by this one act, arguably, more than by any other, the new nation crossed the watershed into the modern world. Today the principle of freedom of religion is generally accepted as an integral part of a democratic constitution.[2]

It was feared at one time that freedom of religion would so divide society that it would spell the end of both religion and society. Most observers now feel that the introduction of religious freedom benefited both religion and society in the end. By making adherence to religion voluntary, it made it more sincere, and a higher percentage of citizens in the United States attend church and synagogue than in any other industrialized country. It also benefited society by providing a secular framework of government, thereby enabling people to offer their loyalty to the state irrespective of their religion.

If religious freedom produces such salutary effects, how could humanity not get to this point sooner? "How could mankind make such an enormous mistake, for such a very long time? What was wrong with the ancient arguments, which were accepted for millennia, apparently without question?"[3] These are interesting questions, but we must resist the temptation of trying to answer them, because the attempt might take us far afield. The question we need to address is rather *how* lack of religious tolerance prevented the emergence of a liberal society. The denial of religious freedom is ultimately a form of authoritarianism, by which the individual is forced to continue to conform to the beliefs of the group. It thus involves the denial of individualism. One way in which this denial proceeds is by the insistence that the children may not deviate in any way from the beliefs and practices of the elders.

The narrative that follows dramatizes this point in a Hindu context.

The name of Prahlāda is a household word among the Hindus, a byword for a devotee of God. The Hindu texts on devotion to God speak of no less than "nineteen attitudes or *bhāvas* which the *bhakta* may adopt towards the deity,"[4] such as those of a servant toward a master, a friend toward a friend, and so on. One such *bhāva* or sentiment involved in this list pertains to the affection felt by a parent for the child, or by the child for the parent, as paradigms of emotional bonding with God. The love felt by the parent for the child is then distinguished from the love felt by the child for the parent. The former is called *vātsalya* and the latter is called *śānta*. Thus *vātsalya bhāva* consists of "the love of the parent to the child. Kausalyā had the Lord Himself as her child in the form of Rāma. The love of Yaśodā to Kṛṣṇa was of the nature of *vātsalya*. *Śānta-bhāva* is the converse of *vātsalya*; it is the feeling of a child to his parent. Dhruva and Prahlāda are the classical examples here. They were the children of God in every sense of the term."[5]

The significance of Prahlāda in the history of Hindu theism is, however, one thing, and its significance for human rights discourse quite another. The two are not unrelated, but the accent falls on different parts of the story. To proceed any further on this line of investigation, however, one needs to know the story first.

The story begins with the incarnation of Viṣṇu as a boar. In this incarnation, Viṣṇu rescued the Vedas from the depths of the oceans to which they had been consigned, and he rescued the world from the oppression to which it was being subjected by the demon Hiraṇyākṣa, by killing him. Now this demon also had a brother, Hiraṇyakaśipu by name, who resented the killing of his brother and wanted to avenge it. To acquire the necessary power to do so, he fervently prayed to Brahmā. Brahmā, much pleased by the rigor and intensity of his austerities, offered him a boon. Hiraṇyakaśipu then specified the boon he would like to receive as follows:

> O my lord, O best of the givers of benediction, if you will kindly grant me the benediction I desire, please let me not meet death from any of the living entities created by you. Grant me that I may not die within any residence or outside any residence, during the daytime or at night, nor on the ground nor in the sky. Grant me that my death not be brought [about] by being other than those created by you, nor by any weapon, nor by any human being or animal.[6]

Hiraṇyakaśipu's wish was granted. Armed with this boon, he began to oppress the followers of God Viṣṇu, not excluding his own son Prahlāda.

At this point we step into the narrative as found in the *Bhāgavata Purāṇa*.

Yudhiṣṭhira said:	O sage divine, O observer of vows! I wish to learn from you why the father began to trouble his own pure and pious son.

Parents, who love their children, may chastise their own recalcitrant sons to teach them a lesson, but they do not punish them like an enemy.

This is all the more odd if the children are obedient, virtuous, and honor the parents.

O Brahmin! This arouses great curiosity in me, O lord! Please remove it—that a grievance may compel a father to try to kill his own son.

Nārada said: The demons accepted the blessed Śukācārya as their chaplain. He had two sons: Ṣaṇḍa and Amarka. They dwelt near the palace of the demon king.

They taught the wise child Prahlāda who had been handed over to them, along with the other demon children of school-going age.

He repeated whatever he heard from the teachers and but in his heart did not approve of the distinction which was drawn between oneself and others, regarding it as false.

O Yudhiṣṭhira! One day the demon king placed his son on the lap and asked him, "Son! Tell me whatever you consider virtuous."

Prahlāda said: O best of *asuras* (demons)! Among the human beings, whose minds are ill at ease because of clinging to what is false, I consider him virtuous who avoids falling into the dark well of domesticity and seeks refuge in Viṣṇu after retiring to the forest.

Nārada said: The demon, on hearing the words of his son, which espoused the views of the rival party, laughed and said: "The minds of the boys is being subverted by the views of the enemies.

The twice-borns should take care of the child properly, so that the mind is not subverted by partisans of Viṣṇu acting in disguise."

The priests of the demons called Prahlāda, who had now been brought back home, and, after praising him gently, asked him in pacifying words:

"Dear Prahlāda. Blessings be on you. Tell the truth. Don't lie. How have you learnt all these contrary things far beyond the other students?

O delighter of the family! Has this different opinion been prompted by others, or did it arise in you spontaneously? We elders are eager to know about it. Tell us."

Prahlāda said: "I bow to that God by whose incredible power the false distinction between oneself and others is drawn by men with deluded minds.

When God becomes favorably disposed toward human beings, the false knowledge that this other person is someone apart for me, the way animals think, is dispelled.

This very *ātman*, difficult to discern and to track down, is perceived with the (false) understanding that it is different between me and others. On this path even the knowers of the Vedas and Brahmā and the rest feel bewildered. But that *ātman* has penetrated my intelligence.

O Brahmin! Just as iron filings are set in motion on their own in the proximity of the magnet, so is my mind spontaneously affected simply by the will of Viṣṇu."

Nārada said: The very intelligent Prahlāda became silent after saying this much to the Brahmins. The pathetic royal servants became angry after condemning him.

"Hay! Bring a stick to beat him with, who has brought bad name to us. This fool is the black sheep of the family and deserves corporal punishment.

This thorn has appeared in the sandalwood of the demon family. This boy is like the handle of the axe called Viṣṇu, which is all set to uproot it."

By uttering threats and in similar other ways, they tried to frighten Prahlāda and instructed him with presentations pertaining to the three goals of *dharma*, *artha*, and *kāma*.

Then, when the master was convinced that Prahlāda had learnt the tetrad of *sāma, dāna, daṇḍa,* and *bheda,* he showed Prahlāda to the king of demons, after he had been bathed by the mother and had put on ornaments.

The demon king greeted his son, who had fallen on his feet, with blessings, and experienced great happiness embracing him for long with his arms.

O Yudhiṣṭhira, he placed him on his lap, smelled his head and moistening the bright face of Prahlāda with drops of tears, spoke as follows.

Hiraṇyakaśipu said: "My dear Prahlāda, tell me something very nice that you have read in all this time, my long-lived son, which you have learnt from your teachers."

Prahlāda said: "Devotion toward Viṣṇu can be offered by human begins in these nine ways: (1) hearing the name of God; (2) chanting the name of God; (3) remembering the name of God; (4) serving the feet of God; (5) making various offerings to God; (6) offering prayers to God; (7) acting as a servant to God; (8) acting as a friend of God and (9) surrendering oneself totally to God.

One who does this to God directly I deem as one who has learned the best that is to learnt."

The lips of Hiraṇyakaśipu began to throb with anger, on hearing these words of his son, and he said to the son of Śukrācārya:

"O bogus Brahmin! What nonsense have you taught to this child, siding with my enemy and dishonoring me, you fool! There are many wicked persons, conniving friends, and hypocritical people in the world, and their crimes become known in the course of time, like the diseases of sinners."

The son of Śukrācārya said:

"O enemy of the king of the gods! What your son has said, he has said without being prompted by me or anyone else. O king! This insight has come to him naturally. Please control your anger and do not blame us."

Nārada said:

On hearing this reply of the master, the king spoke again to his son: "If you have not learnt this from your teacher, wherefrom did you get these strange ideas?"

Prahlāda said:

"They do not think of Kṛṣṇa either on their own or at the instance of others. Therefore all those who lead the domestic life attain darkness on account of lacking control over their senses. Again and again they experience what they have already experienced.

They do not know that their real interests are served by Viṣṇu. They set out to achieve their goals in the outside world under false hopes. They, entangled in strong chords, which characterize the order of God's world, are like the blind led by the blind.

So long as they do not choose to smear themselves with the dust of the feet of the great souls who possess nothing, their minds will not get in touch with God, whose purpose is the removal of every evil."

When the child had stopped speaking in this way, Hiraṇyakaśipu, his soul sunk in darkness, threw the child down on the earth from his lap.

Overpowered with indignation and anger, with his eyes redshot, he then said: "Kill him quickly; he deserves it. Remove him, O demons. This boy is the killer of my brother. This heel has abandoned his own well-wishers and serves the feet of that Viṣṇu like a slave, who killed his uncle (Hiraṇyākṣa).

Or what good will he do for Viṣṇu, this undependable fellow, when he has already given up on the unstinting affection of his parents, although only five years old.

Even another's son, who wishes one well, is precious like a medicine; even one's own son, who does not wish one well, is to be treated like a disease. That part of the body that is injurious to oneself should be excised; by cutting it off, one lives happily for the rest of one's life.

He should be killed in whichever way possible—while eating, lying down, or sitting. He is an enemy posing as a friend, like the wild senses of a sage."

Those demons were thus ordered by their master. They held spears in their hands. They had sharp teeth and fearful faces. Their moustaches and hairs were copper-colored.

They danced to a terrifying beat shouting: "Cut him up, chop him up."

They struck Prahlāda with their spears even as he sat, attacking all the vulnerable parts of his body.

All these attacks on Prahlada proved ineffective, like the good deed of a wicked man, as Prahlāda sat meditating on the supreme *Brahman*, about which nothing can be predicated and on God, the inner self of everything.

O Yudhiṣṭhira, now the king of the demons, alarmed at the failure of this attempt at his life, began with determination to devise other ways of killing him.

He tried to kill him through mighty elephants, poisonous snakes, black magic, by throwing him from mountains, by various tricks, imprisonment, by having poison administered, by starving him to death, through such elements as snow, wind, fire, and water, by having him attacked with mountains. But that demon did not succeed in killing his sinless son and fell into deep thought when he failed to accomplish his goal.

"He has been much abused by me and I devised many ways of killing him. I tried all those treacherous and unethical ways, but he remained unharmed, by his own prowess.

This child is not far from me, yet his mind is not affected. He is fearless like Śunaḥśepa. He will not forget my misdeeds.[7]

This majesty is unfathomable; he is totally fearless; he defies death, indeed by opposing him I may die. Or I may not."

Śaṇḍa and Amarka, the two sons of Śukrācārya, spoke to him in private, upon seeing his bleak and downcast look as a result of his anxiety:

"You have won the three worlds on your own. The mere movement of your brow alarms all the chiefs. Lord! We don't think you should worry about him. One does not think of right and wrong when it comes to children.

Let him be kept tied up with the noose of Varuṇa, so that he does not run away out of fright. The intelligence of a person is affected by age and serving the noble (so he could change his mind). Let this be so until master Śukrācārya arrives."

Saying "so be it" to what the sons of the master had said, and giving them permission to go ahead, he said: "Let him be instructed in the conduct of kings leading the life of householders."

They then, O king, coached the the humble and obedient Prahlāda in *dharma, artha,* and *kāma* thoroughly in proper order.

As he was instructed by the teachers in the three goals of life (*dharma, artha,* and *kāma*), he did not think well of this instruction, because it was shot through by considerations of duality.

When the teachers would withdraw for performing the rites of the householders, he would be called out by other children, who were his friends, when the opportunity arose.

Then the wise Prahlāda, after responding to them with gentle words, spoke to them about the path as a favor with a smile, for he was learned.

Such was his charisma that all of them left their playtoys alone. Their minds had not been influenced by doctrines with celebrate duality.

O best of kings, they sat around him, their hearts and minds fixed on him. Then the demon, the great worshipper of Viṣṇu, full of friendship and compassion, said to them:

"The wise man will start practicing devotion to God even as a child, because birth as a human being, although impermanent, is rare and significant,

A person here should approach the feet of Viṣṇu. For he is the object of every creature's devotion, master of the soul and friend.

O children of the Daitya (demon) family, on account of beings being associated with a physical body, the joys and sorrows of the senses are everywhere experienced as ordained, without any effort on one's part.

One should undertake no effort in this regard—it is only a waste of time. The salvation that comes from the lotus-feet of Kṛṣṇa is not obtained in this way.

Therefore the wise person, while leading a worldly existence, should seek salvation, before one loses ample physical stamina.

A person's life consists of a hundred years, but for a person who has not overcome his senses, it is half of that. For he sleeps futilely at night, sunk in blinding darkness.

The bewildered persons lose twenty years, in childhood and adolescence in play, and another twenty years of the indiscriminating are lost in old age.

The rest of the years of the attached and wayward ones are lost at home, under the powerful grip of insatiable passion and attachment.

How can one, who has not overcome the senses, hope to free himself, when tied down to domestic life with powerful bonds of attachment.

Who can one get rid of longing for wealth, which is even dearer than one's life. The thief, the professional servants, and the merchant even risk their lives for its sake.

How can one lose one's feelings for the private moments spent with one's willing wife and for the tender nothings, attached as one is to the members of one's family by the bond of affection, and loves one's lisping children.

How could one not have feelings—as one remembers them—for one's sons and dear daughters, one's brothers and sisters and one's parents; for one's lovely homes with all sorts of furniture; family wealth, and the animal pets and servants?

How could one give up the various activities one performs, busy as a silkworm, out of desire for more, when all desires have not been met; while thinking highly of the pleasure of mating and eating, how can one feel detached when such attachment is unending?

The heedless person does not see how the opportunity is being lost in spending his life for supporting his family. He is not put off from enjoying family life, although bothered by the three miseries (*ādhidaivika*, *ādhibhautika,* and *ādhyātmika*) everywhere.

His mind is ever engrossed in making money. He knows the sin involved in appropriating the wealth of others, either after death or even in this life. Yet the man with a family does so because he has not overcome his senses and his desires are not satisfied.

O children of demons, even the learned are unable to make ends meet while trying to provide for the family. One who is always distinguishing between what belongs to me and what belongs to others is lost in darkness, like a fool.

Because no one anywhere has been been able to save himself by himself, the poor fellow leads the life of a playboy and is deeply bound to that way of life.

Therefore, O demon-children, give a wide birth to those demons who indulge in sensual enjoyment and approach Viṣṇu, the primal god. He is the desired goal of those who have given up attachment.

O children of the demons, loving God does not take much. He is the very soul of everything and therefore exists everywhere:

In the beings high and low, beginning with immovable objects and ending with Brahmā, in all material manifestations and in the radical elements, in the essential qualities both whether they are in equilibrium or not, there is this one supreme soul, imperishable God, who controls all. He is present in the form of one's innermost self and himself present in visible forms.

He can be described as both that which is pervaded and that which pervades; he is also indescribable because there is nothing else.

He is the supreme lord, whose only form is the form of bliss in which he is experienced. His glory is concealed by *māyā* but shines forth through the *guṇas.*

Therefore show compassion and friendliness to all beings, giving up demonic nature so that transcendent God is thereby pleased.

If that God, the alpha and the omega, is satisfied, what is unattainable? What does one have to do with *dharma* (*artha* and similar goals), which are automatically achieved by the permutation of the *guṇas*? What need to desire liberation? Let us sing his praises whose feet embody the essence.

The threefold classification (of the goals of life), which is said to consist of *dharma, artha*, and *kāma*; self-realization; the three Vedas; the science of law and order; the various schools of economics—I think the truth about this entire corpus of sacred knowledge consists in surrendering oneself to that supreme person, one's intimate friend.

This pure knowledge, not easily accessible, was explained by Nārāyaṇa, the friend of human beings, to Nārada. It may be attained by those who are solely devoted to God, who possess nothing, and whose bodies are smeared in the dust from the lotus-feet of God.

I obtained the knowledge, along with its praxis, of this pure *bhāgavata dharma,* from Nārada, who had seen God."

The Sons-of-Demon said: "O Prahlāda, neither you nor I know of any teacher than these two sons of Śukrācārya, who have charge over us children.

A child dwelling in the ladies quarters is not likely to come in contact with a sage. O gentle one, dispel this doubt (about how you learnt from Nārada) so that we can have confidence in what you say."

Nārada said: That demon, who was a great devotee of God, upon being thus questioned by the sons of the demons, said to them with a smile, remembering my words.

Prahlāda said: "When our father Hiraṇyakaśipu left for practicing penance on the Mandara mountain, the gods launched a mighty attack on the demons.

Indra and others said: 'Fortunately the people have risen against him. The sinner will be consumed by his own sins like a serpent being eaten up by ants.'

Upon coming to hear of their great offensive, the leaders of the demons beseiged by the gods were terrified and fled in every direction.

All of them, eager to save their lives, fled right away, without caring for their wives, sons, wealth, relatives, homes, animals, and household items.

The gods, sensing victory, raided the royal camp, and Indra caught hold of me and my mother, the royal queen.

As she was being carried away terrified and crying like an osprey, by chance the sage saw her on the path.

He said: 'O Indra, you cannot carry away an innocent woman like this. O fortunate one, release this devoted wife who belongs to someone else.'

Indra said: 'The formidable seed of the demon is in her womb. She will remain with us until the child is born, and I will set her free once we get what we want.'

Nārada said: 'He is sinless, great devotee of God right away, a follower of the Infinite and a powerful being; you will not be able to kill him.'

Indra, thus spoken to, out of respect of the words of the divine seer Nārada, left her alone and, after circumambulating her out of love of the Infinite, left for heaven.

Then the sage brought my mother to his hermitage, consoled her, and said: 'My dear, please stay here until your husband returns.'

In this way she lived near the sage, free from fear, until the demon finished performing his severe austerities.

The devout one served the sage with great devotion, for the well-being of the womb that she carried, wanting to be delivered of it come time.

The compassionate sage and master gave instructions to both her and me in the pure and essential knowledge of *dharma*.

In the case of my mother, it was obscured on account of the long interval of time and because she was a woman, but I can still remember it as a special favor from the sage.

And if you have faith in my words, by that faith clear knowledge will come to women and children as it came to me.

■ ■ ■ ■

Nārada said: Now all the children of the demons, upon hearing this description, accepted it an account of its flawless quality, and did not accept what they had been taught by the master.

Then the son of Śukra, upon noticing that their minds were in the grip of that view alone, got alarmed and quickly informed the king.

The body of Hiraṇyakapiṣu began to tremble with rage. He decided to kill his son, rebuking Prahlāda with harsh words that he did not deserve. Looking at Prahlāda, who stood bent in humility, quiet and with folded hands, with an evil and crooked eye, the naturally cruel Hiraṇyakaśipu spoke, hissing like a snake who had been trampled underfoot.

Hiraṇyakaśipu said: "You impudent fool, the destroyer of the family, you wretch. You are obstinate and disobeyed my orders—I am going to send you to hell today.

When I get angry, the three worlds, along with their lords, begin to tremble. Yet before such a one you stand fearless. You fool—on account of what power have you dared overstep my instructions?"

Prahlāda said: "He is not only the source of my power or of yours, but he is the very strength of all those who are strong and of others. All those high or low, or that move or do not, such as Brahmā and others, are under its control.

He is the Lord, he is Time, he is the Strider, he is Vigor, Forbearance, Vitality, Strength, Senses, the Self. He is the universe, the supreme, with his power he creates, maintains, and terminates. He is the lord of the three *guṇas*.

Give up your demonic nature. Steady the mind. There are no enemies apart from an unsubdued self pursuing the wrong path. That is the greatest worship of the infinite.

Some of those, who steal everything away, think that they have conquered the ten directions, without defeating the six enemies first. For one who has conquered his self, who possesses knowledge, and for whom all creatures are equal—for such a virtuous person, how can there be enemies other than those produced by our own delusions?"

Hiraṇyakaśipu said: "You obviously want to get killed now that your boast exceeds all bounds. Those about to die, O fool, begin to prattle nonsense.

This lord of the world other than me, you nitwit talk about—where is he? If he is everywhere, why he is not seen in this pillar? I will chop off your head from your body, who swagger so. Let Viṣṇu protect you today in whom you have sought refuge."

Chastising his son, so devoted to God, in this way with harsh words out of anger, the great demon, of mighty strength, grabbed hold of his sword and, arising from his seat, struck a blow on the pillar with his fist.

My dear Yudhiṣṭhira! At that very moment there was a terrifying sound, as if the very lid of the universe had cracked. When it reached the abode of Brahmā and others, they thought their own abodes had been destroyed.

He was moving toward his son vigorously to kill him, when he heard the unprecedented bang. He could not trace the source of that sound, which had terrified the demon chiefs within the assembly.

In order to prove the truth of the statement of his servant Prahlāda, and the truth of his presence in all things, he appeared in the pillar in the palace in a wondrous form, which was neither that of a human being nor of an animal.

Hiraṇyakaśipu beheld this creature from all sides, which had emerged out of the middle of the pillar. How strange—it was neither a human being nor an animal. He wondered what was this, which had the form of a man and animal.

The form of man-lion thus appeared in front of Hiraṇyakaśipu, as he was examining it. It was very terrifying. The eyes were blazing like molten gold. The flashing mane magnified the face. The teeth looked omnivorous. The razor-like tip of the tongue seemed like a sword in motion. The ears were perked high and were amazingly like a mountain cave. The mouth and nose were flaring. The spaces between the jaws aroused fear. The body seemed to touch the sky. The neck was short and fat. The chest was broad. The waist was short. It was sizzling with hair, white as the rays of the moon. The arms spread out in all directions in a hundred rows, baring nails as weapons. One dared not approach it. It had all kinds of weapons, some unique, some in common use. Its glory caused the demons and *rākṣasas* (ogres) to scatter.

"It seems that Viṣṇu, with his great deceptive powers, has plans to kill me, but what will come of it?" Murmuring thus, the huge demon attacked the man-lion with his club with a roar.

The demon disappeared in the effulgence that was the man-lion, like a moth falling into a flame. This is not strange in relation to that Abode of Goodness, who had formerly swallowed up darkness with his light.

> Then Hiraṇyakaśipu attacked the man-lion and struck him swiftly with a club in anger. But Viṣṇu seized him as he attacked with his club, as Garuḍa might a huge serpent.
>
> The demon slipped out of his hand, playing just like a snake of Garuḍa. The gods who had lost their homes, and the rulers of heavenly planets from the clouds, O Yudhiṣṭhira, did not think well of this.
>
> The great demon thought that the man-lion had lost his confidence because he had eluded his grasp. He, his fatigue gone, then again attacked the man-lion with his dagger and shield, with great speed and force in battle.
>
> Viṣṇu engaged him, as Hiraṇyakaśipu moved up and down moving like a hawk, leaving no opening with his sword and shield, blazoned with moon-spots. The powerful lord caught hold of him, after letting out a loud laugh and a shrill fearful sound, which made the demon close his eyes.
>
> Viṣṇu caught him, who had not been touched by Indra's bolt, threshing wildly at being captured, like a mouse in the grip of a snake, and, placing him on his thighs, at the threshold of the door, tore him apart with ease, just as Garuḍa might rip apart a snake with its claws.
>
> *Bhāgavata Purāṇa VII.4.44, VII.7.16 and VII.8.3 to VII.8.29*

The right to freedom of religion appears to be a fairly straightforward right to begin with, but it can get fiendishly complex if probed further. The selection presented previously had to do with the religious freedom of children, but even here the issue can take on a complexity all its own in no time. Clause (3) of Article 26 of the Universal Declaration of Human Rights reads: "Parents have a prior right to choose the kind of education that shall be given to the children." The word education could easily be construed to include religious education. And, should that be the case, the entire complexion on the case cited earlier changes from one in which the rights of the son, Prahlāda, are being violated into one in which the rights of his father, Hiraṇyakaśipu, are being violated.

This selection, however, helps problematize the question of religious freedom in the Hindu context in an even more suggestive way. Many tributes have been paid to Hindu tolerance, and the term has almost come to mean religious freedom in a Hindu context. Although there is no doubt that Hinduism provides a fertile field for the exercise of religious freedom, one point in this selection deserves special notice if we look upon the gods and the demons as inhabiting *two distinct worldviews.* It is because the demons inhabit a radically different worldview that the worship of Viṣṇu by Prahlāda becomes such a problem for his father, that the father is prepared to take his life. The choice of Viṣṇu by Prahlāda as a deity would not pose the same problem, if the father also inhabited the same worldview. For instance, although it might not be common, it is certainly not extraordinary for the son in a household to adopt Viṣṇu as his chosen deity (*iṣṭadevatā*), although the father worshipped Śiva as his chosen deity, if both the son and the father were living in a family of the *devas*. It is because Hiraṇyakaśipu represents a family of the Dānavas, or demons, who are violently opposed to the devas, that the problem takes on an additional layer.

From this, one can generalize and say that Hindu religious freedom presupposes the same universe of social and legal discourse. If the Hindu community is governed by the same mores and laws, the principle of the *iṣṭadevatā* certainly enshrines religious freedom. An extreme example of this is provided by the fact that, if the Hindu's identity with his or her community is not problematic; one could even choose one's "chosen" deity from another religion. It might raise a few eyebrows, but not much more. It is the difference in the fundamental lifestyle assumptions of the gods and the demons that causes anguish. This imparts special significance to the remark by Udayanācārya (c. 1000) that, although various peoples may follow different systems of philosophies, all Hindus inhabited the same shared world of Vedic sacraments.

Now one is in a position to see why the question of conversion acquires such a sharp salience for the Hindu. As the Hindu sees it, conversion means the adoption of a different set of sacraments in the place of Hindu sacraments, by one who was formerly a Hindu. By "converting" in this manner, the basic assumption of Hindu religious freedom is compromised. If the Hindu accepted Christian or Islamic doctrines while remaining culturally a Hindu, that is, by sticking to Hindu sacraments, the issue of his "conversion" is hardly a problem. It is not even looked upon as conversion.

The problem that human rights discourse poses for Hindus is that the Christian and Islamic communities do not share this Hindu cultural assumption. The Hindu has difficulty realizing that neither the conception of the nature of the relationship between religion and culture in Christianity nor the totalistic conception of religion in Islam square with the Hindu presupposition. Christianity, unlike Hinduism, distinguishes sharply between religion and culture, which are seen as an integrated whole by the Hindu. This distinction allows a person to be a Christian while dwelling in different cultures—from European to Korean. And conversion is thus seen as purely religious phenomenon, whereas a Hindu is not inclined to view it as such, because of the symbiosis between religion and culture in Hinduism. Similarly, the Hindu has difficulty comprehending why the Muslim cannot be a Hindu culturally, while remaining a Muslim religiously, just as a Hindu might become Christian religiously, while remaining a Hindu culturally. The Hindu has difficulty realizing the fact that, because Islam is a total system, it will demand adherence to Islam alone, unlike Hinduism.

Chapter 4

Hinduism and the Right to Property

Western discourse on human rights is often accused of focusing too much on civil and political rights, as opposed to what are called solidarity and collective rights. Our purpose in drawing attention to this fact is not to criticize such a focus, but to draw attention to its historical roots. The early assertions of rights often took the form of protest against the arbitrary behavior of the king, or the state, in relation to the nobles or the individual. The charter of liberties known as the Magna Carta, to which the English barons forced King John to assent at Runnymede in 1215, was in good measure to prevent the arbitrary confiscation of property. Similarly, one of the earliest civil rights of which John Locke (1632–1704) speaks is that of the right to property. It has been surmised that, as the wealth of the merchants increased with the expansion of European mercantile activity over the world, one of the early concerns of these merchants was to safeguard it against its arbitrary appropriation by the state or its representatives. It has been noted, for instance, that "the rights revolution is a story of struggle indeed, the concepts of rights comes from the struggles of the male landholders of England and France to throw off the tyranny of barons and kings and establish rights of property and due process of law."[1]

It has also been similarly noted in the case of the United States that "the right to private ownership of property was certainly deemed fundamental by the framers of our constitution. They entrenched a provision into the Bill of Rights precluding the government from taking property without just compensation."[2]

This right to property, however, is not an unmixed blessing. For instance, "In Massachusetts, private citizens may own their own oceanfront beaches. Many citizens are outraged by the denial of access to what they regard as our collective public seashore. Because of the limited amount of oceanfront in Massachusetts, the value of such beaches has skyrocketed to the point that the state could not now afford to buy them at market value for public use."[3] More generally,

> So when you engage in rights talk, you are committed to a certain kind of individualism. This has its limits. I've mentioned the difficulty rights talk has in focusing on the social and economic inequality that accompanies the competitive individualism of market society. Doing something serious about inequality means infringing on property rights. We hesitate to take this step not just because large capitalists have political power, but also because most of us are property holders ourselves, and we use our power in the political marketplace to resist the taxation necessary to make a redistributive dent in inequality. The problem, in short, is neither individualism nor individual rights. Nor is it capitalism. The chief obstacle to making a dent in inequality is democracy.[4]

Nevertheless, the right to property is crucial for a society to function. The following narrative indicates how the state, even in ancient India, endeavored to respect this right of its humblest citizens.

There seems to be a widely prevalent view that Hindu statecraft is bereft of the concept of human rights, which is often seen to be a gift from the West. This view should be tested against the following account, which is derived from the *Rājataraṅgiṇī*, "a history of Kashmir, written throughout in verse, by Kalhaṇa in CE 1149–50."[5] Its fourth canto describes the following incident, or rather series of incidents, during the reign of King Candrāpīḍa (c. 720 CE).[6]

When [the king] commenced the construction of the temple of Tribhuvanasvāmī, a tanner would not give up his hut, which was situated on the selected site.

He would not allow the site to be measured, under the grip of congenital obduracy, although he was constantly offered money by the officers in charge of the new construction.

They then approached the king and apprised him of the case, but the king took the view that the fault lay with them rather than the tanner.

"What kind of lack of forethought is this that you embarked upon the new construction without first consulting him?" he exclaimed.

"Either stop the work or build elsewhere; am I to compromise my virtue by grabbing hold of someone's land?"

"Who would tread the path of law if we ourselves, who are supposed to be able to sift right from wrong, proceed in a manner which is illegal?"

While the king was talking in this manner, a messenger sent by his council of ministers on behalf of the tanner arrived and said:

He (the tanner) wishes to see the king but sends word that, if it is not proper for him to enter the chamber, he may see the king in the lobby.

He was granted an audience by the king the next day outside the chamber, and the king asked him: "Why are you acting as the only obstacle to a virtuous act?

If you are fond of your house then you may look for an even better one, or accept a large amount of money as an option."

Thereupon the tanner, who, as it were, was measuring the sincerity of the king by the rays emanating from his shining teeth, said to the king who had fallen silent:

"O king, what I am about to say to you comes from the heart, so do not hold it against me as you are the best judge of it.

I am not as low as a dog and you are not as great as Rāmacandra; so why should the councilors be upset by a heart-to-heart conversation between us?

The body of a being, which has come to be born in the world of *saṁsāra*, is made of brittle armour, held together only by the twin clasps of the instinct of self and the instinct of self-preservation.

The body of your highness is resplendent with bracelets, armlets, necklaces, and so on, but we too, who own nothing, are proud of our own body.

My cottage, whose window, if made of the hollow of an earthen-pot, means as much to me as your palace, shimmering in shining plaster, to your majesty.

This little cottage, like a mother, stands witness to the joys and sorrows of my life. I cannot bear to see it razed to the ground.

The pain that a person feels when his dwelling is seized can only be described by a celestial being who has lost his celestial palace, or by a king who has lost his kingdom.

Nevertheless, if you came to my dwelling and asked for it as per the rules of hospitality, then the right thing for me to do would be to offer it to you."

After he had replied in this way, the king went to his home and purchased the cottage for a sum of money. Those who seek bliss do not let pride come in the way.

Then the tanner spoke to the king in his home, with folded hands, as follows: "O king, it is proper that you should yield to another out of righteousness.

Yudhiṣṭhira, the son of Dharma, was tested by Dharma by assuming the form of a dog and so have I, an untouchable, tested your righteousness today.

Hail to you. May you live long to provide a fitting example for your officers by your acts of uprightness."

In this way the king, of stainless character, sanctified the land by consecrating the image of Keśava at Tribhuvanasvāmī.

Rājataraṅgiṇī IV.55–78

This high regard for the right of property is also attested to by an account in which the supernatural element may be excessive for modern taste, but which nevertheless establishes the role of right to property in Hinduism—to which theft poses the chief threat. Kalhaṇa, in discussing the reign of Meghavāhana, provides the following account:

15. The reign of this ruler, though he lived in more recent times, was rendered wonderful by events that surpassed the stories of the first kings.
16. Once when the king was taking recreation in the open, he heard from afar loud cries raised by people in fright: "A thief, a thief here."
17. "Who [is that], who is there? Let the thief be bound!" When the king in anger spoke thus, the loud cries for help ceased, but no thief could be discovered.
18. Again, two or three days later when he was going out, two or three women of divine appearance presented themselves before him praying for safety.
19. When the compassionate [king] had stopped his horse and had promised [to listen to] their request, they with their folded hands raised to the parting of their hair spoke thus:
20. "While you of divine power rule the earth, who could, indeed, O you embodiment of mercy, be in fear of any one else?"

21–24. "When our husbands, the Nāgas, were once covering the sky in the form of clouds, the peasants, who were afraid of the sudden hail-shower and who were agitated in their minds by watching the rich ripe crop of rice, made them, O Lord, cunningly the object of your violent anger. When Your Majesty, hearing the cry of the distressed: 'A thief, a thief,' had angrily ordered their detention, then on your mere command they fell down bound in fetters. May you now have pity on us and show mercy to them!"

25. Having heard this, the king smiled and said, with his face brightened by kindliness: "Let all the Nāgas be freed from their fetters."
26. Upon this order of the king of Nāgas shook off their fetters and, after bowing down before his feet, quickly departed with their families.[7]

The importance attached to property also becomes clear from the fact that Kalhaṇa criticizes the dissolute king Kalaśa (1063–1089) of "seizing the property of those who died without issue,"[8] anticipating Lord Dalhousie's doctrine of lapse!

Another account in the *Rājataraṅgiṇī*, pertaining to the reign of Yaśaskara (CE 939–948), describes in detail how royal attention is drawn to a wrongdoing in relation to property and how the king sets out to remedy it.

14. The officers watching cases of voluntary starvation (prāyopaveś-ādhikṛta), reported a certain person engaged in Prāyopaveśa. When the king had him brought before himself, he spoke:
15. "I was once a wealthy citizen here. In the course of time I became a pauper, through the will of fate."
16. "When my indebtedness had become great, and I was pressed by the creditors, I resolved to throw off my debts and to travel about abroad."
17. "Thereupon, I disposed of all I owed to clear my debts and sold my own mansion to a rich merchant."
18. "From the sale of this great building, I excepted only a well, fitted with stairs, having in view the maintenance of my wife."
19. "I thought that she would live by the rent given by the gardeners, who at summer-time place flowers, betel-leaves, etc., in that very cool well."
20. "After wandering about for twenty years, I have come back from abroad to this my native land with a small fortune."
21. "Searching for my wife, I saw that good woman with a wan body living as a servant in other [people's] houses."
22. "When I asked her, distressed, why she had, though provided with a sustenance, taken to such a life, she told her story."
23. "'When, after your departure abroad, I went to the well, that merchant drove me away, beating me with cudgels.'"
24. "'Then how could I otherwise maintain myself?' After saying this, she stopped. Hearing this, I fell into the depths of grief and anger."
25. "I then began a Prāyopaveśa, but somehow the different judges decided against me, giving on each occasion judgment in favor of the defendant."
26. "In my simplicity I do not know the law, but my life I stake for this: I have not sold the well with the stairs."
27. "Deprived of my property, I die for certain here at your door. Decide the matter in person, if otherwise you have fear of committing a sin."

28. The king, on being thus addressed by him, proceeded to hold court himself and, after assembling all the judges, inquired into the real facts.
29. The judges spoke to him: "This man has been repeatedly dismissed [with his claim] after due consideration. Full of deceit, he does not respect the law and should be punished as a forger of a written document."
30. Thereupon the king read himself the words as they stood in the deed of sale: "The house is sold together with the well [fitted] with stairs."
31. While the councilors cried "From this it is clear," an inner voice of the king, as it were, declared that the claimant was in the right.
32. After apparently reflecting for a moment, the king diverted for a long time the assembled councilors by other very curious stories.
33. In the course of the conversation he took from all their jewels to look at and, with a laugh, drew the ring from the defendant's hand.
34. After, with a smile, asking all to stay thus only for a moment, he retired [into another apartment] under the pretense of cleaning his feet.
35. From there he dispatched an attendant with an oral message to the merchant's house, handing him the ring, so that he might be recognized.
36. Showing the ring, this attendant asked the merchant's accountant for the account-book of the year in which the deed had been executed.
37. When the accountant was told that the merchant required that [book] that day in court, he gave it, keeping the ring.
38. In this [book], the king read among the items of expenditure [an entry of] ten hundred Dīnnāras, which had been given to the official recorder (adhikaraṇalekhaka).
39. From the fact that a high fee had been paid to that person, who was entitled only to a small sum, the king knew for certain that the merchant had got him to write a sa for a ra.
40. He then showed this in the assembly, questioned the recorder whom he had brought up under a promise of impunity, and convinced the councilors.
41. At the request of the councilors, the king granted to the claimant the house of the merchant, together with his property, and exiled the defendant from the land.[9]

Rājataraṅgiṇī VI.14–41

Chapter 5

Hinduism and the Right to Livelihood

The right to property was discussed in the previous chapter. It needs to be carefully noted that the right to property means that the state shall not arbitrarily take away one's property; it does not imply that one has a right to be given property by the state. Crucial to this context is the distinction between negative rights and positive rights. Some scholars have felt this negative definition of rights to be rather narrow. Bhikhu Parekh writes, for instance,

> Each came to be defined in narrow and restricted terms. Thus the right to life was taken to mean the right to be free from physical harm by other men; but not the right to material sustenance without which life is impossible, or the right to be free from unsanitary conditions of work or an unhealthy living environment, or excessively long hours of work—all of which directly or indirectly reduce the span of life. The right to be free from the arbitrary will of others, including the government, and to participate in the conduct of public affairs, did not include the right to be free from the arbitrary will of employers, who remains free to sack their employees or reduce their wages at will. As for the right to property, it meant the right to acquire property and to have if defended against others' interference; and not what it literally meant, the right to (possess at least some) property. We need hardly discuss why only these rights, and not such other rights as personal development, self-respect, employment and education, were emphasized; nor even why they were so narrowly defined.[1]

The situation, however, began to change with the passage of time.

> Another important change occurred in the second half of the nineteenth century. The rights to life, liberty, and property that had so far been emphasized were all rights to *protection*, in the sense that the only things their agents required to enjoy or exercise them were forbearance, or non-interference by their fellow citizens, and protection by the government. In the nineteenth century, social and economic rights were added to the list. Now, obviously, these have a very different character. They are not rights to protection but *provision*—the provision of sustenance, the means of material well-being, employment, and even basic opportunities for personal growth. As such, they required the government to play a positive and active role in economic life. They also imply that, in order to meet the social and economic rights of those in need, citizens should not merely forbear from interference but positively contribute, by taxes and other means, to the resources which a government requires.[2]

The Universal Declaration of Human Rights incorporates both kinds of rights—the negative as well as the positive, those that involve protection as well as those that involve provision. As Mary Ann Glendon points out, the Universal Declaration of Human Rights did not suddenly drop from heaven engraved on tablets, but rather was a milestone on a path on which humanity had already been traveling for at least the past few centuries:

> The Declaration marked a new chapter in a history that began with the great charters of humanity's first rights movements in the seventeenth and eighteenth centuries. The British Bill of Rights of 1689, the U.S. Declaration of Independence of 1776, and the French Declaration of the Rights of Man and Citizen of 1789 were born out of struggles to overthrow autocratic rule and to establish governments based on the consent of the governed. They proclaimed that all men were born free and equal and that the purpose of government was to protect man's natural liberties. They gave rise to the modern language of rights.[3]

It is important to refer to this historical background of the Universal Declaration of Human Rights, because it helps explain a special feature of the modern language of human rights.

> From the outset, that language branched into two dialects. One, influenced by continental European thinkers, especially Rousseau, had more room for equality and "fraternity" and tempered rights with duties and limits. It cast the state in a positive light as guarantor of rights and protector of the needy. Charters in this tradition—the French constitutions of the 1790s, the Prussian General Code of 1794, and the Norwegian Constitution of

> 1815—combined political and civil rights with public obligations to provide relief for the poor. In the late nineteenth and early twentieth centuries, as continental European Socialist and Christian Democratic parties reacted to the harsh effects of industrialization, these paternalistic principles evolved into social and economic rights.[4]

On the other hand, the Anglo-American dialect of rights language emphasized individual liberty and initiative more than equality or social solidarity and was infused with a greater mistrust of government. The differences between the two traditions were mainly of degree and emphasis, but their spirit penetrated every corner of their respective societies.[5]

> The language of human right continued to reflect these two dialects.
>
> When Latin American countries achieved independence in the nineteenth century, these two strains began to converge. Most of the new nations retained their continental European-style legal systems but adopted constitutions modeled on that of the United States, supplementing them with protections for workers and the poor. The Soviet Union's constitutions took a different path, subordinating the individual to the state, exalting equality over freedom, and emphasizing social and economic rights over political and civil liberty.[6]

The right to livelihood as a fundamental human right has yet to gain the salience enjoyed by the right to security of person or the right to freedom of expression. It does find a mention towards the end in Article 23 in the Universal Declaration of Human Rights. The first clause of Article 23 runs as follows: "Everyone has the right to work, to free choice of employment, to just and favourable conditions of work and to protection against unemployment."[7] It should be read with the first clause of Article 25, which reads: "Everyone has the right to a standard of living adequate for the health and well-being of himself and of his family, including food, clothing, housing and medical care and necessary social services, and the right to security in the event of unemployment, sickness, disability, widowhood, old age or other lack of livelihood in circumstances beyond his control."[8]

What is remarkable in the narrative that follows is the early recognition of the *positive right to sustenance* in the Hindu ethos, which took longer to crystallize in the Western context.

The following incident from the *Araṇya* or *Vana Parva* of the *Mahābhārata* seems to bear on the right to livelihood, especially if it is pared down to its most irreducible—the right to food. The setting is provided by the gods Indra and Agni (Fire) setting out to test the virtuous conduct of King Śivi.

Indra turned into a hawk and Fire into a dove and went to the sacrifice. The dove took to the king's thigh out of fear of the hawk and, seeking refuge, it nestled there terrified.

The hawk said: O king, all kings declare you to be virtuous. Then why do you wish to act in a contrary manner? I am suffering from hunger and this is my ordained food. Do not begrudge it out of excessive fondness for virtue, for thereby you discard virtue itself.

The king said: O mighty bird! This bird has come to me panic-stricken, craving for its life after being frightened by you, as a refugee. Don't you see, O hawk, that it would be supremely unrighteous of me not to offer refuge to this dove, who has come to me seeking it. O hawk, this dove has come to me trembling and desperate, to save its life; it will be despicable to abandon it.

The hawk said: O king, all creatures come into being through food, they live on food and thrive on it. It is possible to survive for long by giving up one's dear possessions but it is not possible to go on living for long without food. If I am deprived of my food, O king, my life will leave my body, never to return. O virtuous one, if I die, so will my wife and offspring; you will cause many deaths by trying to save the life of a dove. That course of virtuous conduct, which in effect obstructs the course of virtue, is not virtue, it is vice. O truthful one, true virtue is universal in its application. O king, weigh the pros and cons of the opposite courses of action and adopt that virtuous course of action that oppresses none. Having weighed the merits and demerits of a course of action, choose that which is more meritorious.

The king said: O best of birds, you speak benevolently. You, king of birds, with lovely feathers, are without doubt well-versed in virtue. And you speak wonderfully and virtuously. It seems to me that there is nothing you don't know; then how come you consider it virtuous to surrender someone who has sought shelter? O bird, you do all this for food; you can have it in other ways and even more of it. A steer, a boar, a deer, or even a buffalo can be provided for you, or whatever else you want.

The hawk said: O king, I shall not eat a boar or bull or deer of various kinds. What have I to do with their meat? I shall have the food ordained for me, O king. Release this dove. It is long-established practice that hawks eat doves. You know the true path, O king; do not try to climb up a banana tree.

The king said:	You are honored by hosts of birds; I rule over this prosperous kingdom of the Śibis. I shall, O hawk, give you whatever you want, but not this dove, which has come to me seeking my shelter. O best of birds, tell me how I may make you desist from this course and I shall do it, but I shall not hand over the dove.
The hawk said:	If you are so fond of the dove, then cut off a piece of your flesh and weigh it against the dove. When your flesh equals the dove in weight, then give it to me. That will satisfy me.
The king said:	O hawk, I deem it a favor that you make such a request. I shall give you my own flesh of equal weight.
	That supremely virtuous king cut off his own flesh and weighed it with that of the dove. But the dove weighed more on the balance. The king then cut off other pieces of his flesh and offered them. When he found that even then there wasn't enough flesh to equal the weight of the dove, he himself mounted the scale.

Mahābhārata III.130.19-20 to III.131.30

There are specific references to the king providing sustenance to the Brahmins in the *Rājataraṅgiṇī* (VIII.75), but also more generally to people in apparent distress (I.131). Provision for water is also referred to (IV.244).

The significance attached to the right to livelihood may be gathered from the fact that the means of livelihood of each *varṇa* is usually specified within Hinduism. Thus, according to the *Manusmṛti*, various duties were assigned to the four *varṇas*, which upon inspection turn out to be closely associated with their means of livelihood. Thus according to *Manusmṛti* (88.91):

> To Brahmins, he assigned reciting and teaching the Veda, offering and officiating at sacrifices, and receiving and giving gifts. To the Kṣatriya, he allotted protecting the subjects, giving gifts, offering sacrifices, reciting the Veda, and avoiding attachment to sensory objects, and to the Vaiśya, looking after animals, giving gifts, offering sacrifices, reciting the Veda, trade, moneylending, and agriculture. A single activity did the lord allot to the Śūdra, however: the ungrudging service of those very social classes (10.74–80).[9]

How the "right" to livelihood emerges in this context may be demonstrated by examining the course of action recommended for the first and the last *varṇa*, namely the *brāhmaṇa* and the *śūdra*, when they are unable to make the ends meet by pursuing the duties allotted to them above. The following verses of the *Manusmṛti* are relevant here (XI.16–22):

> Likewise, when a man has not eaten during six mealtimes (6.19n), at the seventh mealtime he may take from someone who performs no rites, keeping to the rule of leaving no provisions for the next day, and taking it from his threshing floor, field, or house, or from any place where he can find something. If the man questions him, however, he should confess it to him.
>
> A Kṣatriya must never take anything belonging to a Brahmin; if he has no sustenance, however, he may take what belongs to a Dasyu or a man who neglects his rites. When a man takes money from evil persons and gives them to the virtuous, he makes himself a raft and carries them both to the other side. The wise call the wealth of those devoted to sacrifice the property of gods; the possessions of those who do not offer sacrifice, on the contrary, is [sic] called the property of demons.
>
> A righteous king should never punish such a man, for it is because of the Kṣatriya's foolishness that the Brahmin is languishing with hunger. After finding out who his dependants are and enquiring into his learning and virtue, the king should provide him with provisions for a righteous livelihood from his own house. After providing him with a livelihood, he should protect him in every way, for, by protecting him, the king receives from him one-sixth of his merits.[10]

Although the Brahmin is not specified in the first two verses, most scholars take them as applying to him on account of the context.[11] Note that the Brahmin is permitted to take what he can to keep body and soul together. In the last paragraph previously cited, the king is supposed to provide for his livelihood as well. In other words, a Brahmin *in extremis* has the *right* to help himself and also has the *right* to be supported by the king.

Patrick Olivelle seems to suggest that the first paragraph may apply not just to any Brahmin but to a twice-born hermit.[12] If such is the case, once again it becomes the *right* of the hermit to help himself. The concept of the right, in this case, emerges in the context of the *āśrama* scheme as well.

In relation to the *śūdra* the situation is as follows:

> If a śūdra was unable to maintain himself and his family by serving dvijas, he was allowed to maintain himself by having recourse to crafts such as carpentry or drawing or painting pictures etc. Nārada (ṛṇadāna 58) allowed him to perform the work of kṣatriyas and vaiśyas in times of distress. Yāj. (I.120) also says that, if unable to maintain himself by the serve of dvijas,

> the śūdra may carry on the profession of a vaiśya or may take to the various crafts. The *Mahābhārata* allowed a śūdra who could not maintain himself by the service of higher varṇas to resort to the avocation of a vaiśya, to rearing cattle and to crafts.[13]

The provision in the *Manusmṛti* in such a situation is somewhat more restrictive (X.99–100):

> When a Śūdra is unable to enter into the service of twice-born men and is faced with the loss of his sons and wife, he may earn a living by the activities of artisans—that is, the activities of artisans and various kinds of crafts the practice of which best serves the twice-born.[14]

These *in extremis* situations are covered by the term *apad-dharma* in the law books, which also provide a list of ten occupations, which all the *varṇas* may resort to in a crisis. Thus *Manusmṛti* (X.116) declares:

> The ten means of livelihood are: learning, craft, employment, service, cattle-herding, trade, agriculture, fortitude, begging, and lending on interest.[15]

The exercise is in danger of becoming somewhat arid at this point. The fact, however, that it has been undertaken with not one but two goals in mind may arouse the interest of the reader. Its first goal was to document the importance attached to the right to means of livelihood in Hinduism, but the second goal might interest the reader even more. It requires a word of explanation.

The claim has often been made that India, or even Asia, lacked a concept of rights and, in fact, *had no word for it.* The prior exercise renders this view questionable, for we see clearly that, in the context of *āpad-dharma* or "rules for times of adversity," the most appropriate way of describing the situation is in terms of rights. Thus the *brāhmaṇa* has the right in such times of royal support, and the *śūdra* has the right to follow the vocations of a *vaiśya,* for instance.

The fact that the same word *dharma,* usually translated as duty, may also mean right in certain contexts should not come as a surprise, given the strong correlation between the two. As an example of double meaning, one may also wish to consider the English word "minister," which describes both the head of a *religious* congregation and a member of a cabinet, a more *secular* meaning.

Chapter 6

Hinduism and the Rights of Children

The rights of children gained recognition in the discourse on human rights in the West only gradually. In relation to children, for instance, the Universal Declaration of Human Rights says: "Parents have a prior right to choose the kind of education that shall be given to their children" (26.3) and "that along with motherhood" childhood "is entitled to special care and assistance" (25.2). Locke deals with these issues in a very different spirit. Contextualizing his views with those of Hart and Melden, Stanley I. Benn notes:

> There is, however, another class of special rights, which Hart mentions but which he does not reconcile with the equal right to freedom—namely, rights arising from special but apparently non-consensual relations. Locke dealt with the same example of such a right that Hart uses, that of parents to the obedience of their children, by making rationality a condition for the right to freedom and by making the parents' right consensual as soon as children reach the age of reason. It would be more difficult, perhaps, to reconcile with the equal right to freedom the instance suggested by Melden—namely, a parent's right to special favourable consideration from a child—which, it seems, is neither consensual nor extinguished merely by the child's growing up.[1]

Moreover, the Universal Declaration of Human Rights also states (25.2): "All children, whether born in or out of wedlock, shall enjoy the same *social* protection" (emphasis added), a concept that perhaps assumed clarity after Locke.

The discourse on human rights has steadily expanded with the passage of time. At one time, the concept of human rights effectively applied only to some men. Gradually it came to include all men. Then it was extended to include women's rights,[2] and these days there is increasing talk of children's rights.

This extension of human rights discourse to include children constitutes an extension of human rights discourse in a direction congenial to Hinduism. The conception of Kṛṣṇa as a child-god in the legends about him is not irrelevant here, in that it represents a fundamentally positive orientation toward the child. The same positive orientation is also perhaps reflected in the fact that "the cult of the child Kṛṣṇa made a special appeal to the warm maternity of Indian womanhood; and even today the simpler women of India, while worshipping the divine child so delightfully naughty despite his mighty power, refer to themselves as 'the Mother of God.'"[3]

The story of Aṇī-māṇḍavya as found in the *Mahābhārata* is unusual in many ways, but, toward the end, it takes an interesting twist, which seems to make it rights-friendly so far as children are concerned. At the very least, it shows an awareness of the rights of children.

The background to the story is provided by the fact that, even though Vidura is treated as an incarnation of *Dharma* in the *Mahābhārata* epic, his social status in the epic is that of a *śūdra,* the lowest of the four *varṇas* that are said to constitute Hindu society.[4] This anomaly is then explained as the outcome of a curse. This leads King Janamejaya, to whom the account is being narrated by sage Vaiśampāyana, to ask:

Janamejaya said:	What did Dharma do as a result of which he came to be cursed? O sage, on account of whose curse was he born in the womb of a *śūdra*?
Vaiśampāyana said:	There was a famous *brāhmaṇa* named Māṇḍavya, who was persevering, virtuous in every way and firm in truth and austerity. That great *yogī* stood with his arms upraised at the root of a tree at the entrance to the *āśrama*, observing the vow of silence. While in this way he had been practicing austerities for a long time, O best of Bharatas, robbers carrying their plunder arrived at the hermitage, chased by many guards. They placed the loot in his hovel and, when the guards approached, concealed themselves terrified. Then the posse of guards that was following the robbers arrived on the scene and saw the sage. They then asked the sage, who was thus standing, which

way the robbers went so that they may chase them down. The sage, however, O king, did not utter a word either way. Then the officers of the king found the thieves and the goods as they searched the hermitage. The guards became suspicious of the sage. They detained him and produced the robbers before the king. The king passed the sentence that he should be killed with those thieves. He was fixed on a stake by the executioners, who did not recognize him. The guardsmen then returned to the king with the plunder, after hoisting the sage at the stake.

The sage did not die, even though he hung on the stake for a long time without food. He held on to life and summoned the seers. The seers were greatly mortified by the sight of the sage suffering on the stake. They returned in the night after turning into birds and, displaying such powers as they possessed, asked: O Brahmin, we wish to know what sin you have committed. Then that tiger among the sages replied to the seers: "Whom should I blame? I alone am guilty."

The king, upon learning of the sage, went to him with his councilors and appeased him thus: "If I have done something wrong out of confusion or ignorance, then I beg your forgiveness, please do not be cross with me." The sage was pleased when thus spoken to by the king, and the king then had him lowered. When he had him lowered down from the top of the stake, they did not succeed in freeing him from it entirely. A piece of it was lodged in his flesh, and it had to be cut off at the end. The sage then moved about with the stake embedded in him and was thereafter known among the people as Aṇīmāṇḍavya—or Māṇḍavya with the stake.

That Brahmin, who knew the ultimate reality, then went to the mansion of Justice (Dharma) and, upon seing Justice (Dharma) seated, taunted him as follows:

> What was that deed unwittingly committed by me as a result of which such havoc was wreaked on me? Tell me the truth of the matter quickly, behold the power of my austerity.

Dharma said: You stuck blades of grass in the tails of insects (as a child). O sage, you have suffered this result as a consequence of that action.

Aṇīmāṇḍavya said: Your punishment is out of proportion to the offense. Therefore, O Dharma, you will be born as a human being from the womb of a *śūdra*. I am now laying down the limit in the world for the fruition of actions. *Until a child reaches the age of fourteen, no action of his shall be deemed a sin; but thereafter it shall be considered an offense.*

Mahābhārata I.101.1–26[5]

Concern with the rights of the child can also be identified in some other accounts, which otherwise seem fanciful. Two accounts in the *Rājataraṅgiṇi* are of particular interest from this point of view. Both are rich in moral comment. According to the first account, King Meghavāhana prohibited the killing of all living beings as an act of virtue. But this led to an unexpected outcome. The child of a Brahmin fell ill, and he attributed the fever to the fact that goddess Durgā was not being propitiated by him through the required animal sacrifices.

82. Then as time passed by, some aggrieved Brahman bringing his pain-stricken son lamented at the king's gate:
83. "Without giving to Durgā the animal oblation which she desires, I who have no other issue, shall lose my son to-day from fever."
84. "If you persist in the [law of] not-killing and do not preserve this [my son], O protector of the earth, then who else could appear to me the cause of his death?"
85. "May you yourself, O guardian of [all] castes, give here judgment as to how great a difference there is between the life of a Brahman and of an animal!"
86. "O mother earth, those kings who killed even ascetics in order to gain the life of Brahmans have now disappeared."
87. While the Brahman spoke contemptuously these harsh words in his grief, the king, the destroyer (hara) of the pain of the afflicted, long reflected in this manner:
88. "Aforetime I made the rule that living beings should not be killed. Why should I even for the sake of a Brahman do what I have recognized as ruinous?"
89. "If the Brahman [youth] should die today, leaving me as the immediate cause [of his death], there too would be a case of extreme sinfulness, that of [causing] distress intentionally."
90. "My soul tossed about by doubts finds no rest on [either] side, like a flower that has fallen into a whirlpool at the junction [of two streams]."
91. "If I then satisfy Durgā by offering up my own body, I righteously preserve the lives of [these] two as well as my vow."
92. Having thus meditated for a very long time, the king, who was ready to sacrifice his own body, dismissed the Brahman with the words: "Tomorrow I shall do what pleases you."

93. During the night Durgā restored the Brahman's son to health and [thereby] prevented the king who was anxious to offer up his body [from carrying out his intention].
94. We feel embarrassed in thus recording also of this king of recent times these and other acts, which cannot be believed by common people.
95. However, those who proceed by the [righteous] way of the Ṛṣis, are also in their compositions not dominated by subservience to the hearer's notions.
96. When this king died, after ruling the earth for thirty-four years, the whole world was as if deprived of the sun and light.

Rājataraṅgiṇi III.82–96[6]

It is noteworthy that the author, Kalhaṇa, is no less conscious of the supernatural element in verses 94–95 than we are, but there are several points of interest in this passage. There is first the moral dilemma created by the impending death of the son. Apparently the king had decided to resolve the dilemma at the *personal level* by offering himself as a victim, although he was happily prevented from going through with his resolution by a positive turn of events—the recovery of the son. But the issue still remains valid at a general and theoretical level. How is one to proceed when personal rights and collective rights come into conflict? The mythical flavor of this dilemma should not blind us to its immediacy. Perhaps the point will gain in clarity if the same dilemma is presented in a modern guise, as in the following incident; described by John B. Carman: "Once in the mid-nineteenth century a group of Brahmins representing the hierarchy of a temple in Tirunelveli, in the extreme south of India, came before the British magistrate with a serious complaint. The outcastes with the traditional duty of pulling the car had become Christian, and they now refused to pull the car, with the result that the entire festival could not take place."[7] How this case relates to the issue on hand becomes clear as the point is developed by Professor Carman:

> It was generally British policy to respect the customs of Hindus and other religious groups, but in this case the British magistrate had a serious problem. How, he asked the Brahmins, could he compel the outcastes to perform a vital service for a religion to which they no longer belonged? To this the Brahmins had a prompt and emphatic reply. It does not matter, they said, what your personal religious convictions are, or what the personal feelings of the outcaste servants are. The duty to which they were born, their dharma, is to provide physical labor to the rest of the community, and your duty as a ruler is to force them to do their duty. Otherwise the procession

> cannot proceed, and the dharma of the temple will be disregarded. If the ritual order is upset in this way, the deity will be displeased and will withhold the rains. Your duty as ruler is to ensure the prosperity of the entire people through the timely arrival of the monsoon rains, and that maintenance of cosmic order depends on the ritual order of the temple, including the pulling of the temple car.[8]

Crucial to the issue now was the reaction of the British magistrate:

> The British magistrate declined to act on that complaint, but it was not because British law in India paid no attention to Hindu notions of law, including moral and religious duties. Indeed, the British went to a great deal of trouble to seek out manuals of traditional law, both Hindu and Islamic, in some cases to translate them into English and in a great many cases to adjust British law to the Indians' own sense of what was fair and just. In this case, however, the magistrate also felt an obligation to the outcastes, who by becoming Christians had assumed new religious duties, including what might be called the negative duty of not participating in Hindu festivals. What that magistrate was doing, whether he realized it or not, was interpreting dharma as a self-imposed obligation by morally free agents aware of and responsible for their own choices. It may well have been impossible for any British magistrate in the nineteenth century, anywhere in the world, to do otherwise. Yet this was a profound change from the traditional notion of dharma as a differentiated duty built into the very nature with which a particular group of beings is born and related to a vast system of natural duties embracing all classes of beings in the world. Failure to live according to one's own caste dharma would not only produce bad karma that would affect one's station in life in a future birth; it would also upset the present order of nature, leading to floods, or in South India still more frequently, to droughts.[9]

The reader might wish to recall how King Meghavāhana in the *Rājataraṅgiṇī* sought to resolve the issue in terms of *individual sacrifice.* The modern resolution was different: it was in terms of *individual rights.*

One also notices in the account how the Brahmin refers to the vast difference "between the life of a Brahman and that of an animal" whose sacrifice the king had prohibited, so that the issue of animal rights also emerges, to be pursued elsewhere in this book. At this moment it is the allusion to a similar crisis during the rule of the King Rāma—associated with the ascetic Śaṁbūka, an account also discussed later in this book—that is relevant. The point to be retrieved from this tangled skein of myth is this: the focus on the sanctity of the life of Brahmin, which makes the death of a Brahmin child so heinous, may have to be reassessed from a perspective that emphasizes the rights of a child. The victim in these previously mentioned cases is a Brahmin child, and, although the accent has often been on Brahmin when the expression is used, the time may be ripe to shift in on the child. Once the matter is viewed from this angle, the protest of the father takes on the complexion of a condemnation of infant mortality in a welfare state.[10]

It could be argued that in this case that there is some scope for ambiguity. It is not entirely clear whether the precise center of concern is (1) the fact of the child's *brahminhood*; (2) or the fact of his being a child, or (3) both. It could be further argued that, in the actual narrative in the *Rāmāyaṇa* itself, it is the fact that the boy is a Brahmin that is important to the narrative. However, an extrapolation of the concern to the boy *per se occurs within the tradition itself*, as illustrated by Bhavabhūti's *Uttararāmacarita.* In the Second Act of this play, a Brahmin is said to confront Rāma with his dead boy. At that time, Rāma is *not* depicted as reflecting that "a *brāhmaṇa* or a *brāhmaṇa's* son has died therefore I am to blame" but rather that "untimely death only occurs on account of the misconduct of the king and therefore I am to blame" (*tato na rājāpacāramantareṇa prajāsvakālamṛtyuḥ sañcartītyātmadośaṁ nirūpayati karuṇāmaye rāmabhadre*).[11]

The example cited as follows is free of such ambiguity, which relates to moral concern regarding the life of the child in yet another episode in the *Rājataraṅgiṇī*. It is known as the story of Varuṇa and pertains to King Meghavāhana.

30. While his army was resting there comfortably in the shade of the palm groves, for a short time he thought in his mind over a device to reach the other terrestrial isles (dvīpa).
31. Then he heard from near a wood on the shore a distressed person's cry for help: "Even under Meghavāhana's rule I have been slain."
32. As if he had been struck in his heart by an arrow of heated iron, he quickly moved to that spot accompanied by his royal parasol.
33. Then he saw before a temple of Caṇḍikā (Durgā) a man with his face turned downward who was being killed by some barbarian troop leader.
34. "Shame upon you for this misdeed, you senseless person!" When thus threatened by the king, the barbarian in terror communicated to him the following:
35. "My little son here, O king, hurt by disease, is on the point of dying. This deed, the deities have declared, would bring him some small relief."

36. "If this [propitiatory] sacrifice is prevented, he dies on the spot, and know you that the whole band of his relatives lives only while he lives."
37. "You protect, O Lord, a friendless man brought from the depth of the forest. Why do you take no heed of this child with whom many persons are connected?"
38. Then the high-minded [king], distressed by these words of the barbarian and the terrified look of the victim, spoke thus:
39. "O Kirāta, do not be despondent. I myself save your son who has many relations, as well as this victim, who is without relatives."
40. "I make my own body an offering to Caṇḍikā. Strike boldly at me. May these two persons live!"
41. Thereupon the barbarian, who was astonished by the nobility of soul [shown] by that [king] of wonderful mental courage and who felt thrilled, thus addressed him:
42. "O Lord of the earth, while you strive after too great compassion, some kind of mental error arises in your heart."
43. "Why do you show disregard for that body [of yours], which ought to be protected without hesitation even at the cost of [all] lives in the three worlds, and which is destined to enjoy the earth in happiness?"
44. "In their thirst for life, kings regard neither honor nor fame nor riches nor wives nor relations nor the law nor children."
45. "Therefore, O protector of your subjects, show favor, do not take pity on this victim. While you live, may this child and these [your] subjects also live!"
46. Then the ruler of the earth, eager to sacrifice himself and paying worship to Cāmuṇḍā, as it were, with his brilliant teeth, which glistened as [if they were] an oblation (argha), spoke thus:
47. "What concern have you, forest dwellers, with the enjoyment of the nectar of righteous conduct? Those who live in the deserts know not the delight of bathing in the Gaṅgā."
48. "You go too far, O fool, in your obstinate endeavor to frustrate my desire of buying imperishable fame with this body, which is sure to decay."
49. "Speak not another word. But if you should feel [too much] pity to strike [yourself], why cannot my own sword effect the purpose?"
50. Eager to offer up his body, he drew himself his sword after these words to cut off his head.
51. As he was about to strike, his head was covered with divine flowers and his arm held back by one of divine form.
52. Then in this state he saw before himself a person of heavenly appearance, but neither Caṇḍikā nor the victim nor the Kirāta nor the boy.

53. Thereupon the divine person spoke to him: "O you who are like the moon of the middle (terrestrial) world, and the embodiment of compassion, know that I am Varuṇa who has been subdued by [your] courage."

Rājataraṅgiṇī III.30–53

The mythical embellishments of the story should not obscure the central point—that a child's life is at stake. It is in order to prevent it that a propitiatory sacrifice is performed and that the king is willing to stake his life to save that of the child and the intended victim.

Chapter 7

Marriage and the Rights of Women: Śakuntalā

Modern human rights discourse gives the right of marriage to all men and women, Article 16 of the Universal Declaration of Human Rights reads:

(1) Men and women of full age, without any limitation due to race, nationality, or religion, have the right to marry and to found a family. They are entitled to equal rights as to marriage, during marriage, and at its dissolution.
(2) Marriage shall be entered into only with the free and full consent of the intending spouses.
(3) The family is the natural and fundamental group unit of society and is entitled to protection by the society and the state.

We are concerned, in the narrative that follows in this chapter, with clause (2) in particular. The consideration of this clause in the Hindu context is complicated by two features of marriage as found in Hinduism: (1) the classification of marriage into eight types and (2) the conception of *kanyādāna*, which is explained in this chapter.

According to a pervasive classification of marriages in Hinduism, a marriage is classified as conforming to one of the following eight types:

(1) Brāhma: It involves the marriage of a duly dowered girl to a man of the same class by due ceremony.
(2) Daiva: In this case a householder gives a daughter to a sacrificial priest as a gift.
(3) Ārṣa: Here, the gift of a cow and a bull is involved.

(4) Prājāpatya: In this form the father simply gives the girl away, exhorting both husband and wife to lead the pious life.
(5) Gāndharva: This form of marriage is brought about by the mutual consent of the two parties.
(6) Āsura: This describes marriage by purchase.
(7) Rākṣasa: This describes marriage by capture.
(8) Paiśāca: This involves the seduction of a girl while asleep, mentally deranged, or drunk.

Out of these eight forms of marriage, it is the fifth form—the *gāndharva*—that is explicitly based on mutual consent of the partners; one forms the impression that, in the preceding forms, parental consent or even initiative is a key element. Although the sanctity of these other preceding forms of marriage is emphasized, it should be noted that, despite its unorthodox character, the *gāndharva* form of marriage was respected and, according to some, even the indigenous name for India—*Bhārata*—may derive from the product of such a union.

It is here that the concept of *kanyādāna* becomes a key element in the situation: according to this concept, the parents earn enormous merit by giving away their daughter in marriage. It has been pointed out for instance that

> A marriage under the Hindu law is a sacred covenant. In a Hindu marriage, the bridegroom has to promise that he will look after his wife. On the other side, the bride also promises that she will be faithful to her husband. In the approved form of marriage the essence is the transfer of the gift (kanyadan) by the guardian.[1]

The question can also be raised: "Does it amount to a contract between two men then, as representatives of two joint families? The irksome conceptualization of the bride herself as a mere gift has led to protests about how callously Hindu tradition allows women to be treated as a piece of property, to be given and received in marriage."[2] The charge has been met in various ways, by alluding to the historical circumstances that might have created such a situation, or by drawing attention to the spiritual and religious significance of marriage in Hinduism,[3] but these overlook a crucial factor—that in a *gāndharva* marriage the girl gives herself away.

The following excerpt describes the meeting of Duṣyanta and Śakuntalā and how it culminates in their marriage. The key point to bear in mind, from the point of human rights, is the right of the bride to give herself away in marriage (of the type known as *gāndharva*). This is a key point, because, traditionally, a bride is given away; hence one could argue that it is the right of the father, or the parents, or the guardian to give away the bride. But in the extract that follows, the epic introduces us to a situation in which the bride gives herself away.

It could of course be argued that this applies to only one of the eight forms of marriage—the *gāndharva*—and therefore the right is limited in scope. We would, as students of human rights, do well to remember in this context that what we regard as *human* rights nowadays were often first articulated as the right of a special class. Thus safety of person, a right enjoyed by all today, has its origins in the right of personal safety that the nobles were able to secure from the king, a right which ultimately broadened out into the right to safety of all persons against the state.[4]

The reader might wish to note two more points: (1) that Viśvāmitra is described as a *kṣatriya* who became a *brāhmaṇa*—even gatecrashed into being one (I.65.29)—and (2) that the various forms of marriage are also capable of being combined, a possibility not ordinarily entertained (I.67.13).

The selection is an extended one, for the account builds toward a climax. There are two other reasons for including it *in extenso*, one literary, the other historical. The love, marriage, and ensuing encounter between Duṣyanta and Śakuntalā is a theme that recurs in the history of Sanskrit literature, constituting the plot of a well-known play of Kālidāsa, entitled *Abhijñāna-Śākuntalam*. The product of their union, Bharata, who also goes on to become a *cakravartī*, or a universal monarch, is much celebrated in Hindu lore, and, according to one view, India's name for itself, namely Bhārata, may be traced to him.

The setting is classical. King Duṣyanta is out on a royal hunt.

Vaiśampāyana said:	The long-armed one, going forward alone leaving his ministers behind, did not see the sage, who observed his vows strictly, in the hermitage. Not finding the sage in a hermitage, which was, as it were, empty, he cried aloud, "Who's here," making the forest resound, as it were. Upon hearing his call, a young maiden, beautiful like goddess Lakṣmī, came out of the hermitage, dressed like an ascetic. The dark-eyed one, on seeing the king, quickly welcomed him and paid him homage. She offered him a seat and water for washing the feet and inquired about his health and well-being. After having honored him in this way and inquired into his health, she said with a smile: "What may I do next?"

The king, duly honored, spoke thus to the maiden, who spoke sweetly and who possessed a perfect body: "I have come to pay my respects to the honorable sage Kaṇva. My dear! Tell me where the venerable sage has gone, O pretty one."

Śakuntalā said: "Venerable father has gone from the hermitage to fetch fruits. Please wait a while; you will see him as soon as he returns."

The king, not seeing the sage and addressed in this manner, looked at her who had lovely hips, a beautiful appearance, and a sweet smile, and who shone forth as it were with the glamor of her body, her austerity, and her pious restraint, and who was endowed with beauty and youth: "To whom do you belong, O one with attractive hips, and what are you doing in the forest? O pretty one, where are you from, so young and so beautiful? O auspicious one, I have fallen in love with you at first sight. I wish to know about you. Tell me." The maiden, thus spoken to by the king in the hermitage, said these sweet words to the king with a laugh: "Duṣyanta, I am the daughter of the venerable sage Kaṇva—the wise, righteous and famous ascetic."

Duṣyanta[5] said: The venerable sage, who is worshipped by the world as a revered lord, is a celibate. Even *dharma* itself may swerve from its course, but never a sage with strict vows. O fair one, how could you be his daughter? A great doubt arises in me in this matter, please remove it.

Śakuntalā said: Learn truthfully, O King, how I came to be the daughter of the sage. Once a seer came and raised questions about my birth. Listen, O king, to what the venerable sage told him.

In days of yore, Viśvāmitra performed such immense austerities that they became unbearable for Indra, the lord of the gods. Fearing that the sage, burning with ascetic power, might cause him to fall from his station, the terrified Indra spoke therefore to Menakā as follows:

O Menakā! You excel all divine damsels by your divine qualities. O blessed one, the great ascetic Viśvāmitra, shining like the sun and performing awesome penances, makes my heart shudder. O Menakā with comely waist! This Viśvāmitra is your burden, who is disciplined, redoubtable, and engaged in intense austerities. Go and seduce him, lest he make me lose my position. Obstruct his austerities; please do as I say. O one with fetching hips, seduce him with beauty, youth, sweetness, dalliance, smiles, and talk, and turn him away from austerity.

Menakā said: The great effulgence and brilliance of the venerable one never fades away. And you yourself know how prone to anger he is. If you yourself feel alarmed by the brilliance, austerity, and anger of the great-souled one, would I not feel the same way? He separated the venerable Vasiṣṭha from his sons; although born a *kṣatriya,* he became a *brāhmaṇa* by force; the sacred unfathomable river he caused to flow with copious waters so that he could have a bath is known in the world by the people as Kauśikī (so named after him). When Mataṅga, the royal sage, became a hunter, Viśvāmitra supported his wife in those terrible times of yore. When the time of famine had passed and Mataṅga returned to the hermitage, the lord caused the river named Pārā to flow. And when Mataṅga himself, well-pleased, performed a sacrifice there, then, out of fear of Viśvāmitra, you yourself went to partake of the *soma.* O Indra! He angrily created a family of constellations, as a challenge to the constellations from *śravaṇā* onward. Such are his deeds, and this upsets me mightily. O lord, tell me how to act in such a way that I do not arouse his indignation. He can burn up the worlds with his power, he can shake up the earth with his foot, he can quickly crush Mahāmeru into a ball and twirl it. How can a mere girl like me even go near him who has conquered his senses, who is so austere and blazes forth like fire? How could I dare to touch him? O king, his face blazes like fire, the sun and the moon are pupils of his eyes, and his tongue is like death. Would someone like me not be alarmed when even Yama, Soma, the Great Seers, all the Sādhyas and the Vālakhilyas stand in awe of him. O king, now that you have asked me, I shall of course approach the sage, but, O king of the gods, think of ways of protecting me so that I may accomplish your task. O lord, may wind expose my skirt when I am playing and may, by your grace, Cupid act as my helpmate. May fragrant winds blow from the forest when I set out to seduce the sage. "So be it," he said, and, when the matter had been settled, she set out for the hermitage of Viśvāmitra.

Śakuntalā said: Thus spoken to, Indra ordered the wind accordingly, and then Menakā, accompanied by wind, took off. Now Menakā of lovely hips, somewhat nervous, saw Viśvāmitra performing penance, scorched by ascetic fervor. She greeted him and started sporting near the sage. Wind carried away her skirt, light like moonlight. The fair one fell to the ground quickly, trying to catch hold of her skirt, bashfully smiling. The great sage saw Menakā nude, clutching her skirt, lusting, and young and beautiful beyond words. Then the sage desired union with her on seeing her beauty, falling prey to passion. He invited her and she responded, for no blemish attached to it. Both of them spent a long time together in the forest, enjoying themselves as they wished; however, it seemed but like a day. Menakā gave birth to Śakuntalā, born of the sage, on a level spot in the Himālayas, with the Mālinī river flowing around. Then Menakā left the baby on the banks of Mālinī, now that her task was accomplished, and quietly slipped back to the court of Indra. The birds covered that baby, lying in the remote forest infested with lions and tigers, from all sides. The birds protected the daughter of Menakā lest the flesh-eating carnivores kill the young baby in the forest.

When I went to rinse my mouth I saw her lying in the trackless forest, surrounded by birds. I brought her along and adopted her as my daughter, for three kinds of legal fathers have been spoken of in that order: one who gives one life, one who saves one's life, and one who nurtures one. And I gave her the name Śakuntalā because she had been safeguarded in the forsaken forest by birds (for which a Sanskrit word is *śakunta*).

O friend, in this way is Śakuntalā my daughter and blameless Śakuntalā looks upon me as her father. This is what my father told the sage who asked about my birth. O king, this is how I came to be the daughter of Kaṇva. Not knowing my father, I consider Kaṇva as one. O king! I have narrated to you what I had heard as I heard it.

Duṣyanta said: O blessed one, the way you tell it, it is obvious that you are a princess. O one with beautiful hips, marry me. Tell me what I may do for you. A necklace of gold, fashionable clothes, golden earrings, sparkling gems from many countries, O pretty one—these I shall get for you right away—as well as breastplates and furs. May my entire kingdom be yours. Be my wife, pretty one. O you who are so beautiful, marry me by the rite of *gāndharva*. O one with lovely thighs, this form of marriage is considered the best.

Śakuntalā said: O king, my father has gone out of the hermitage to fetch fruits. Please wait for him. He will give me away to you.

Duṣyanta said: O blameless one with beautiful hips, I would like you to love me and live with me. My heart is set on you. One is one's relation; one is one's own refuge. One can give oneself away lawfully.[6] Eight forms of marriage are acknowledged as legal: (1) *brāhma*, (2) *daiva*, (3) *ārṣa*, (4) *prājāpatya*, (5) *āsura*, (6) *gāndharva*, (7) *rākṣasa*, and (8) *paiśāca*. Manu himself has described their characteristic features in proper order. The first four are recommended for *brāhmaṇas*; O blameless one, the first six are legal for the *kṣatriya*. For the kings, the *rākṣasa* form is also acceptable, and the *āsura* form for *vaiśyas* and *śūdras*. Three of the five are lawful and two unlawful. *Paiśāca* and *āsura* should never be indulged in. This is how one should proceed lawfully. Such is the course of *dharma*. *Gāndharva* and *rākṣasa* forms are valid for *kṣatriyas*, either in combination or separately, without a doubt. O fair lady, you desire me and I desire you; you can become my wife through the *gāndharva* form of marriage.

Śakuntalā said: If this is the right way and if I am my own master, then, O best of Pauravas, this is my condition for bestowal, O lord. Promise me truly, as I speak to you in private, that the son born of me shall succeed you. O king, he will be the prince regent. State this to be so. O Duṣyanta, if it be so, then we can make love.

"So be it," the king replied to her without hesitation. "O one with a chaste smile, I shall moreover take you to my city, for you deserve it, O one with comely hips. I am telling you the truth." Having spoken thus, the royal sage lawfully grasped her, whose movements were flawless, by the hand and lay with her. Having assured her, he left, saying repeatedly: "I shall send the army in full force to get you, and bring you to my own palace escorted by it." The king left, having made this promise to her, wondering how the venerable ascetic Kaṇva would react to what had happened. He returned to his city thinking thus. Within moments of his having left, Kaṇva arrived in the hermitage, and Śakuntalā did not approach him out of embarrassment. The great ascetic Kaṇva, who was gifted with divine knowledge, came to know it all through his divine sight. He was pleased and spoke to her as follows:

You possess royal pedigree. The union you entered into with a man today ignoring me does not constitute a transgression of the law. For a *kṣatriya*, the *gāndharva* form of marriage is said to be the best,[7] which may be entered into without ritual on the basis of mutual attraction, O Śakuntalā. Duṣyanta, whom you have accepted out of love, is pious, righteous, and the best of men. Your son is going to be a high-souled and powerful being, who will rule over the entire earth bordered by the oceans. When the high-souled one will embark on the course of world conquest, he will be irresistible. Then she said to the sage, who was resting after she had washed his feet, put down his handbag, and stocked the fruits: "Please be favorably disposed toward that excellent man I have chosen as a husband and toward his ministers."

Kaṇva said: O fair lady, I am indeed happy for you. Ask a boon from me for him such as you wish.

Śakuntalā asked that the imperial stability and probity of the Paurava line be preserved, wishing well for Duṣyanta.

Mahābhārata I.65 to I.68.33

This excerpt is helpful for revisiting two central social sites in Hinduism in the context of marriage: (1) the concept of the types of marriage and (2) the concept of *kanyādāna.* In terms of the first, it showcases the *gāndharva* form of marriage, the one that comes closest to corresponding to what in India is called "love marriage" (presumably as distinguished from an "arranged marriage"). In terms of the second, it allows the basic feature of *kanyādāna,* usually understood as the giving away of the daughter in marriage by the parents, to be reconstrued as the giving away of the daughter by herself. The potentially revolutionary significance of such a reconfiguration should not be overlooked, because, even in the supposedly liberal West, the bride is still given away in marriage.

Nor are the two contexts unrelated. It is the *gāndharva* form of marriage (in which the parties to the marriage meet each other without the mediation of a third party or parties) that creates the social space for semantically reconfiguring *kanyādāna.*

That a girl should give herself in marriage is not as far-fetched as it sounds. There are verses even in the *Manusmṛti* (IX.89–91) according to which a maiden may, under circumstances, seek out a groom for herself, to whom she may well then offer herself by herself. A maiden is *not* supposed to take the ornaments her family might have in mind for her, if she chooses a husband on her own, according to the *Manusmṛti* (IX.92).]

Chapter 8

Marriage and the Rights of Women: Sāvitrī

Sāvitrī is often held up as the model of traditional Hindu womanhood. Such traditional Hindu womanhood is often associated with male child preference, early and arranged marriages, and a tradition of blind devotion to the husband, of which the practice of Satī might be considered an extreme example.

The actual details of the life of Sāvirtī as depicted in the *Mahābhārata*, however, are anything but. She is born to a couple who are practicing austerities, praying for a *male* child. Then her marriage is not arranged by her parents. She arranges her own marriage. Finally, when her husband dies, she does not get ready to commit Satī. She doesn't even think of it. She pursues the ruler of death, Yama, until he frees her husband.[1]

It is ironical that such a figure should have become the patron saint of the kind of norms associated with the subordination of women. One should begin by taking note of her name, *Sāvitrī*, which is the name of the holy Vedic mantra through which the *male* offspring is initiated into Vedic studies in classical Hinduism.

Some readers may find the long conversation between Sāvitrī and Yama irksome. They might wish to consider the possibility that here we have a countermodel for the wife who commits Satī. A woman is said to secure benefits for both her family and her husband by committing Satī, benefits that are sometimes said to even extend to seven generations in the past and in the future. The scale involved here is more modest and involves only the future. But Sāvitrī does secure the well-being and continuity of both her own and her husband's family. The suggestion that we have here a countermodel for Satī is strengthened by the frequent use of the word *sat*, and various formations of it, in the dialogue between Sāvitrī and Yama, perhaps hinting that Sāvitrī is a *satī* in her own right—a very different kind of *satī,* who, instead of accompanying her husband into the beyond as proof of conjugal fidelity, insists on saving her husband from the jaws of death itself by the power of conjugal fidelity.

Two other aspects of the situation deserve attention from the point of view of modern human rights discourse. As noted earlier, the *Universal Declaration of Human Rights* emphasizes that men and women of "full age" should enter into marriage and that they should do so with "full and free consent."[2] The reader will note how the second condition is met in the narrative as one reads through it, but, given the widespread impression about "child marriages" in India, the fact that the spouses in the account are of "full age" should also be fully borne in mind. The reader might also find the following remarks helpful as he or she settles down to read the narrative:

Mani Ram Sharma (1993: 57) rightly states that there is no fixed age prescribed anywhere in the texts regarding the marriage age of Hindu males. A few samples of texts demonstrate the plurality of Hindu perceptions of this subject. Manusmṛti 9.88–91 (tr. Bühler 1975: 343) suggest:

> 88. To a distinguished, handsome suitor (of) equal (caste) should (a father) give his daughter in accordance with the prescribed rule, though she have [sic] not attained (the proper age).
> 89. (But) the maiden, though marriageable, should rather stop in (the father's) house until death, than he should ever give her to a man destitute of good qualities.
> 90. Three years let a damsel wait, though she be marriageable; but after that time, let her choose for herself a bridegroom (of) equal (caste and rank).
> 91. If, being not given in marriage, she herself seeks a husband, she incurs no guilt, nor (does) he whom she weds.

Such statements, found in a text that is constantly cited as a prototype of obnoxious anti-women positions taken by traditional Hindus, call for a rather drastic reconceptualization of scholarly assumptions about ancient Hindu thinking and practice as regards marriage and sexual relations. Far from suggesting a law of compulsory early marriage, these *Manusmṛti* verses make it quite clear that early marriage may be preferable, but finding a suitable groom for one's daughter is a more important consideration than the age of the bride herself.[3]

Yudhiṣṭhira said:	O great sage! I do not grieve for myself, nor for my brothers, nor the loss of kingdom, as much as I do for Draupadī. We were

saved by her when harassed by evil people during the gambling match. Then she was forcibly abducted by Jayadratha from the forest. Has any woman been seen or heard of formerly as devoted to her husband and as great as Draupadī?

Mārkaṇḍeya said: King Yudhiṣṭhira! Listen to the glory of women of distinguished background and how such distinction was attained by Princess Sāvitrī.

There ruled in the country of Madra a pious king, devoted entirely to virtue, who respected Brahmins and those who sought his refuge; who was true to his word, and who had subdued his senses. He was a sacrificer, a liberal donor, competent, loved by his urban and rural subjects, ever engaged in securing the good of all. His name was Aśvapati. With advancing age he began to feel depressed and undertook severe austerities for the sake of obtaining progeny. He ate little at appointed times, remained chaste, and subdued his senses. That best of kings offered oblation a hundred thousand times with the Sāvitrī mantra and ate sparingly only every sixth time. He spent eighteen years observing this vow. Goddess Sāvitrī, pleased with him at the completion of the eighteenth year, revealed herself to the king, stepping out of the fire-altar with much delight. The boon-giving goddess then spoke to the king as follows: "O king, I am pleased with your chastity, purity, restraint, self-control, and complete devotion to me. O Aśvapati, king of Madra, ask for any boon you want. You should never falter in doing the right thing."

Aśvapati said: I virtuously adopted this course for the sake of obtaining progeny. O goddess, may I have many sons who will extend my lineage. If you are pleased with me, O goddess, then this is what I choose as my wish. The Brahmins tell me that to continue one's line is one's supreme duty.

Sāvitrī said: I have already spoken to Brahmā on your behalf for a son, knowing well your desire. By the grace of the self-created Creator, O gentle one, a brilliant *daughter* will soon be born to you. You should not say anything on this account under any circumstances, for pleased with you I say so in place of Brahmā.

Mārkaṇḍeya said: "So be it," the king acknowledged the words of Sāvitrī and implored again "Let it be so soon." Then Sāvitrī disappeared and the king returned to his palace. The king, well-pleased, continued to live in the kingdom, ruling over his subjects virtuously. After some time had passed, the devout eldest queen became pregnant. O best of Bharatas, the seed grew in the queen, the princess from Mālava, the way the moon waxes in the bright fortnight. Come time she gave birth to a daughter whose eyes were like lotuses, and the delighted king performed the rites for her. She was the affectionate gift of goddess Sāvitrī; she was obtained by offering oblations to Sāvitrī, so the king and the Brahmins named her Sāvitrī. The princess grew up like goddess Lakṣmī in human form, and in due time the girl became an adolescent. When people saw her who was like a golden statue as it were, with a slim waist and broad hips—they thought that they were seeing a divine maiden. She had eyes like lotus leaves and she shone forth with brilliance, but no one would marry her; they were intimidated by her brilliance.

Then she fasted, washed the head ritually, worshipped the gods, made offering in the fire, and made the Brahmins recite duly on an auspicious lunar day. Then she collected the remaining flowers and approached her high-souled father, like Lakṣmī incarnate. After bowing at her father's feet and offering the remaining flowers, she stood besides her father with folded hands. The king felt sore distressed at seeing his divinely beautiful daughter in the prime of youth, yet without a suitor.

The King said: My daughter! It is time to give you away in marriage, but no one listens to me. Choose a husband worthy of yourself on your own.[4] Present the man you wish to marry to me, and, after making inquiries, I shall give you away. Choose what you want. As I have heard in the books of law recited by Brahmins, so you too, blessed one, hear from me as I spell it out: a father who does not give his daughter away in marriage, a husband who does not approach his wife, and a son who abandons the mother after her husband has died—all are reprehensible. Lose no time in searching for a husband after having heard me speak thus. Act in such a way that I may not be reproached by the gods.

Mārkaṇḍeya said: Having spoken thus to the daughter, he deputed his old ministers to accompany her in her travels and urged her: "Proceed." She, confident but bashful, saluted her father's feet and, acknowledging her father's orders, set out without hesitation. She traveled to the attractive hermitages of the royal sages, seated on a golden chariot, surrounded by old ministers. There she saluted the feet of all the worthies distinguished by age and went through all the forests systematically. She travelled through many a region, distributing largesse in all the holy places among the prominent Brahmins.

Mārkaṇḍeya said: O descendant of Bharata! Now the king of Madra was sitting in the assembly hall, conversing with Nārada who was visiting him, when Sāvitrī returned to her father's palace, along with the ministers, after having visited all the places of pilgrimage and the hermitages. Upon seeing her father seated along with Nārada, she bowed with her head at the feet of both of them.

Nārada said:	Where has your daughter been, O king, and where is she coming from? Why have you not given away the young girl to a husband in marriage?
Aśvapati said:	It was for this very purpose that I had sent her and she has returned. O divine sage! Hear now what she has to say about the husband she has chosen for herself.
Mārkaṇḍeya said:	She, being urged by her father to "describe in detail" and acknowledging the words of the divine sage, spoke as follows: "There is a devout *kṣatriya* Śālva king, known as Dyumatsena, who later on turned blind. After he had lost his eyes and while his son was still a child, he was deprived of his kingdom by a former enemy who was a neighbor, when he found the opportunity. He left for the forest along with his wife, accompanied by the dear child. Residing in the great forest, he performed severe austerities, observing great vows. His former son has grown up in the hermitage. [His son] Satyavān is the right match for me. I have chosen him as my husband in my heart."
Nārada said:	O King, Sāvitrī has done something terrible in choosing virtuous Satyavān, without knowing all the facts. His father speaks the truth, his mother speaks the truth, therefore the Brahmins conferred on him the name of Satyavān. As a child he was fond of horses, and he would make horses of clay and also paint them, so he came to be called Citrāśva.
The King said:	Is he bright and intelligent, that prince? Is he forgiving and brave, that Satyavān, and does he please his parents?
Nārada said:	He is brilliant like the sun and intelligent like Bṛhaspati. He is heroic like Indra and forgiving like the earth.
Aśvapati said:	Is the prince generous? Does he honor Brahmins? Is he handsome and generous? Is he pleasing to look at?
Nārada said:	In giving according to his capacity, he is like Rantideva Sāṅkṛti, in honoring the Brahmins and in truthfulness, he is like Śibi Auśīnara. He is pleasing as the moon. He is handsome like the Aśvins. The son of Dyumatsena is strong, self-controlled, kind, brave, honest, and the master of his senses. He is friendly, ungrudging, modest, and wise. He is always straightforward and steady; he is so described by those advanced in austerities and conduct.
Aśvapati said:	Venerable sir! You describe him as endowed with all kinds of virtues. Do point out his defects, if he has any.
Nārada said:	Satyavān suffers from only one blemish so far, none else. His life will run its course within a year when he will cast off his body.
King said:	O Sāvitrī, fair lady, go and choose someone else. This one shortcoming of his makes short work of all his virtues. As the

venerable Nārada has said, who is honored even by the gods: his short life will end in a year when he will cast off his body.

Sāvitrī said: Only once is property divided, only once is a daughter given away in marriage, only once does one say "I give," these three acts are performed only once. I have chosen my husband once for all—be he long-lived or short-lived, with or without virtue. I shall not choose another. I have made up my mind, then expressed my resolution with words, and I shall follow it up with action. My resolute mind is my authority.

Nārada said: O best among men, your daughter Sāvitrī has firmly made up her mind. She cannot be made to deviate from that course in any way. The qualities found in Satyavān are not to be found in anyone else. I would like you to give your daughter away to him.

King said: I shall act without hesitation upon the truth spoken by the venerable one. You are my guru and venerable lord.

Nārada said: May the giving away of your daughter in marriage proceed without a hitch. I leave now and bid you all well.

Mārkaṇḍeya said: Wondering about what had been said about the giving away of his daughter, the king collected all the articles required for the wedding. Then, on an auspicious day, he summoned all the elders, Brahmins, the sacrificial priests, and the domestic priests and set out with his daughter. The king, having reached the holy forests wherein the heritage of Dyumatsena lay, approached the royal sage on foot along with the Brahmins. There he saw the great king sitting on a cushion of *kuśa* grass under a *śāla* tree, but blind. The king paid due homage to the royal seer and presented himself in measured words. The virtuous one offered him a seat and a cow, and then one king asked the other king the reason for his coming, and the other king informed him fully about his intention, his mission pertaining to Satyavān.

Aśvapati said: O royal sage, I have a comely daughter, Sāvitrī by name. Please accept her as your daughter-in-law as per law, you who know the law.

Dyumatsena said: We have lost our kingdom, dwell in a forest, and follow the regulated life of ascetics. How will your daughter put up the inconvenience of living in a hermitage in a forest? She does not deserve this.

Aśvapati said: I and my daughter are aware of the joys and sorrows that may or may not come to pass. You should not speak like this to someone like me. O king, I have come here of my own choice. Do not kill my hope. Please take friendship and affection into account. I approach you with love in every wise. Do not turn me down. An alliance between us is appropriate. Please accept my daughter as your daughter-in-law and Satyavān's wife.

Dyumatsena said: I had cherished an alliance with you even earlier, but then I thought: "I have lost my kingdom." What you propose now is something I had formerly wanted on my own. Let it be fulfilled today. You are a welcome guest of mine.

Mārkaṇḍeya said: The two kings then called all the Brahmins and the residents of the hermitage and had the marriage duly solemnized. Aśvapati, after giving his daughter away with well-deserved dowry, returned to his palace, brimming with happiness. Satyavān was delighted to have a wife who excelled in every way, and she was delighted at having gained the husband she wanted. After her father left, she put away all the ornaments and put on bark garments and saffron robes. She satisfied everyone with her service, her virtues, her affection, her restraint, and by attending to all their wants. She satisfied her mother-in-law by taking physical care of her and all her garments; and the father-in-law by performing worship and by restrained speech. In the same way, she made her husband feel contented by sweet speech, skill, calmness, and personal attention. O descendant of Bharata, some time passed in this way, as the virtuous couple lived in the hermitage practicing austerities. As for Sāvitrī, she kept thinking about what Nārada had said day and night, whether sitting or lying down.

Mārkaṇḍeya said: Then, after much time had elapsed, the moment arrived, O king, when Satyavān was meant to die. Sāvitrī, as she kept count of each passing day, always kept in mind the statement made by Nārada. That lady undertook a vow of three nights' duration and kept standing day and night, keeping in mind that he was to die on the fourth day. The king became distressed when he heard this resolve of the bride. He arose and said to Sāvitrī consolingly: "O princess, the vow you have undertaken is severe in the extreme. It is exceedingly difficult to remain in the same position for three nights."

Sāvitrī said: Dear father, do not feel distressed. I shall carry through my vow. It is undertaken with resolve; resolution is its cause.

Dyumatsena said: I dare not ask you to break your vow. The only proper thing for me to say is that may you made good on your resolution.

Mārkaṇḍeya said: The high-minded Dyumatsena became silent after saying so. And Sāvitrī stood there like a piece of wood. The night of the morning on which the husband was to die, Sāvitrī spent standing, sore distressed, O best of Bharatas. "Today is the day," she thought and lit the fire, and, even though the sun had risen only four cubits, performed the forenoon rites. Then having honored all the Brahmins, elders, mother-in-law, and father-in-law in order of seniority, she stood demurely with folded hands. All the ascetics and all the residents of the hermitage, wishing

Sāvitrī well, blessed her that she may never be widowed. Sāvitrī, deep in meditation, accepted the words of the ascetics in her mind, musing that it might be so. The princess, waiting for the hour and the moment, felt extremely sad, thinking of the prediction made by Nārada. O best of Bharatas, then the father-and-mother-in-law spoke to her, when she was all by herself, out of affection as follows.

Father- and mother-in-law said: You have fulfilled your vow as prescribed. It is time to eat. Then do what needs to be done next.

Sāvitrī said: I shall eat when the sun has set after my desire has been fulfilled. Such is my heart's resolve; I have made this covenant.

Mārkaṇḍeya said: With Sāvitrī having spoken thus so far as eating was concerned, Satyavān left for the forest, placing the axe on his shoulder. Sāvitrī said to her husband: "You must not go alone. I shall come with you. I cannot bear to leave you."

Satyavān said: My dear, you have not trod in the forest before and the path is difficult. You are weak with fasting, how will you manage to walk?

Sāvitrī said: I am not weak from my fast and don't feel exhausted. I am eager to go, so please don't stop me.

Satyavān said: If you are eager to come, then I shall do what you want. But take leave of my parents, so that I don't get blamed.

Mārkaṇḍeya said: That lady, who had undergone the great vow, approached her father- and-mother-in-law and said: "My husband is going into the forest to gather fruits. I would like to have your permission, my lady, and of my father-in-law, to accompany him. I cannot bear to be apart. Your son has set out for the sake of the parents and the fire-altar. He could have been prevented from going to the forest for some other reason, but not in this case. It is just under a year and I haven't ventured out of the hermitage. I am all eager to see the forest in full bloom."

Dyumatsena said: Ever since Sāvitrī was given by her father as a bride to us, I do not recall her ever making any request of us. Let the bride have what she desires. Go, O daughter, but do not come in the way of Satyavān.

Mārkaṇḍeya said: That glorious woman went forth with the permission of both, laughing along with the husband but sad at heart. The lady with large eyes saw the colorful and lovely woods on all sides, echoing with the sound of peacocks. Satyavān sweetly pointed out to Sāvitrī the holy rivers and the large mountains covered with flowers. That blameless one, watching her husband in all these situations, thought of him as dead, as it were, at the time. She followed her husband with soft steps, remembering the words of the sage, her heart cleft in two, as it were, awaiting the hour.

Mārkaṇḍeya said: With the help of his wife, the strong husband filled his case with fruits and then began to chop wood. He broke out into a sweat as he chopped wood, and the exertion involved gave him a headache. He came to his wife exhausted and said: "My head aches from the exertion, and my limbs and heart feel faint. O one of measured speech, I feel unwell. My head feels as if it is pierced with spikes, and, O blessed one, I want to lie down. I can't stand any longer."

Sāvitrī approached and embraced her husband and sat down on the surface of the earth, with his head in her lap. Then, thinking of the words of Nārada, the poor woman calculated the day, the hour, the time, and the moment.

In a mere moment she saw a person wearing yellow, with a turban, stout of body and effulgent like the sun. He had dark, white and red eyes, he held a noose in his hand, and looked terrifying. He stood by the side of Satyavān looking at him. On seeing him, she rose with a start, slowly put down the head of the husband, and, with folded hands, spoke thus, with a trembling heart, feeling utterly crushed. "I know you are a god because your body is superhuman. Tell me if you will, O divine being, who are you and what do you want?"

Yama said: O Sāvitrī, you are devoted to your husband and practice asceticism. Therefore I am going to talk to you, O good woman. I am Yama. This husband of yours, Satyavān, the prince, his life has come to an end. I will tie him up and carry him along. This is what I plan to do.

Mārkaṇḍeya said: O venerable one! The lord of death spoke to her in this way and then proceeded to describe in detail what he was going to do to her dear husband. "He is devout, handsome, and possesses many virtues. He deserves better than to be taken by my servants; therefore I have come myself." Then Yama forcefully extracted a being of the size of a thumb with his noose from the body of Satyavān. The body then became lifeless, without breath, comatose, motionless, and repulsive to look at. Yama, tying him up, began to walk in the southern direction. The great and devout Sāvitrī, of perfect vows, followed Yama, beside herself with grief.

Yama said: Sāvitrī, go back and perform the obsequies. You have done your duty by your husband. You have gone as far as you can.

Sāvitrī said: I shall also go where you go and take my husband. This is the immemorial law. Nothing can obstruct me on account of the austerity I have performed, the service I have rendered to the elders, my love for my husband, the vow I undertook, and

because of your good offices. The sages who know the truth say that a person with whom you have walked seven steps becomes a friend. Keeping such friendship in mind, I wish to say something, please listen to me.
Many masters of the soul in the forest dwell and practice virtue and spiritual exercises,
With full knowledge they proclaim virtue,
Therefore the sages regard virtue to be supreme.
Virtue stands alone, according to the sages and all who follow that path.
I do not seek anything else besides,
For the sages regard virtue to be supreme.

Yama said: Return. I am pleased with your speech,
Distinguished by clear enunciation and reason.
Choose a boon other than your husband's life
O blameless one, I shall grant any wish of yours.

Sāvitrī said: My father-in-law, in the hermitage,
Has lost his kingdom and now lives there.
May he regain his vision and be strong,
May he shine forth like the sun, by your grace.

Yama said: O blameless one, I grant your boon in full;
It will come to pass as you have asked.
You seem tired by traveling,
Return, go lest you get too tired

Sāvitrī said: How can I feel tired close to my husband,
For my husband is my firm recourse.
My place is where you take my husband,
O lord of gods, please listen to me again.
Even a single encounter with the sages is highly desirable,
And friendship is said to be even more so.
The company of the wise is never fruitless;
Therefore one should live in the midst of sages.

Yama said: The words spoken by you to me
Are cordial, wise, and salutary.
Again choose a boon other than Satyavān's life;
Fair lady, choose a second boon.

Sāvitrī said: The kingdom that my wise father-in-law lost,
May the king obtain his kingdom.
May my father-in-law never stray from his duty.
I choose this as the second boon.

Yama said: He will soon regain his kingdom.
The king shall not stray from his duty.
I have fulfilled your wish, O princess,
Return, lest you get too tired.

Sāvitrī said: You bind the creatures in accordance with law,
And then carry them after binding them so, and not arbitrarily.
O god, that is why you are called the Restrainer,
Please listen to what I have to say.
Absence of ill-will toward all creatures in thought, speech, and action; compassion and charity: these are eternal values cherished by the sages. This world is such that people follow these to the best of their ability. But the sages even show mercy to their enemies if approached by them.

Yama said: Like water to the thirsty
Are the words spoken by you.
Again choose a boon other than Satyavān's life.
Good woman, choose the boon you desire.

Sāvitrī said: My father has no sons.
May my father have a hundred sons, my siblings,
Who will extend the family line.
I choose this as the third boon.

Yama said: Good woman, may your father have
A hundred splendid sons to extend the family line.
I have fulfilled your wish, O princess.
Return. You have come a long way.

Sāvitrī said: It is not far if I am close to my husband,
But my mind runs even farther.
Even as you walk along, please listen
To my ready words as I speak to you.
You are the majestic son of Vivasvān—the sun.
That is why the wise call you Vaivasvata.
The creatures are pleased by your restraint and virtue.
In that, O lord, consists your virtuous rule.
A person cannot even repose as much confidence in himself as he can have in the virtuous. Therefore all specially seek to love the virtuous.
Confidence indeed arises out of goodwill in all creatures. Therefore a person reposes special confidence in the virtuous.

Yama said: The words you have spoken, beautiful woman,
I have not heard from anyone else, good woman.
They please me; other than Satyavān's life
Choose a fourth boon and go your way.

Sāvitrī said: May a child born to me and Satyavān
Make the families of both of us flourish.
A hundred strong and powerful sons,
This I choose as my fourth boon.

Yama said: A hundred strong and powerful sons
O frail one, will be born to you and delight you.

O princess, lest you get fatigued,
Return. You have come a long way.

Sāvitrī said: The virtuous are always virtuous.
They are not affected by depression and grief.
A meeting with the virtuous is never fruitless.
The virtuous are not afraid of the virtuous
The virtuous guide the sun, in truth.
The virtuous uphold the earth by their spiritual power.
The virtuous know the course of the past and the future.
O king, the virtuous do not come to grief among the virtuous.
The virtuous do good to others without expecting anything in return,
Taking this to be the eternally noble course of action.
The grace of the virtuous never fails.
One loses neither wealth nor honor among them.
Because such is the set course of the virtuous.
Therefore the virtuous are the guardians of all.

Yama said: As you go on speaking what is pious,
Pleasing, polished, and pithy;
So my devotion to you increases.
O firm in vows, choose any peerless boon.

Sāvitrī said: *You have made no exception with this stipulation,*
As you have in the other cases,[5] O bestower of pride.
I choose life for Satyavān,
For without my husband I am as good as dead.
I do not want happiness without my husband.
I do not want heaven without my husband.
I do not want prosperity without my husband.
I do not plan to live without my husband.
A boon for the birth of hundred sons
Was given by you, but you carry my husband away.
I choose life for Satyavān.
Your own words have to come true.

Mārkaṇḍeya said: "So be it," said Yama and released the noose. Pleased to the core, the lord of Law spoke to Sāvitrī as follows:

"O good woman, here I release your husband. You are the delight of the family. He is in good health. Take him along. He will attain his goal.

Mahābhārata III.277 to III.281.55

Chapter 9

Marriage and the Right of a Woman to Choose Her Husband

This is the third segment that addresses this crucial human right of women—to choose their own husbands. A key factor here is, of course, the age at which the marriage is performed. In a situation of child-marriage, such a right could hardly be exercised. Even Mahatma Gandhi had an arranged marriage. So, to sharpen the question: Did women of full age have the right to choose their husbands?

One discovers in the narratives pertaining to Śakuntalā and Sāvirtī that they did, but because the epic deals largely with the warrior class or caste, the question arises whether women of other castes also exercised this right. In this respect, the evidence from the *Kathāsaritsāgara* is of some interest. The *Kathāsaritsāgara* is a Sanskrit version, prepared by Somadeva in the eleventh century, of that famous repository of folklore in Prakrit, the *Bṛhatkathā* of Guṇādhya, usually placed in the early centuries of the Christian era.

One such story pertains to a wealthy merchant, Ratnadatta, who had a daughter, Ratnāvatī by name, but no sons. The story narrates how she resisted all the efforts of her parents to get her married. Then one day she saw a thief being led to his cross through the streets, and fell in love with him and even mounted the pyre with him. A. L. Basham remarks as follows on the story: "Stories such as this puzzle the social historian. If the texts on the Sacred Law have any relation to real life it is quite incredible that a girl of good class in the 11th century should have been given such freedom by her parents, or should even have thought of legally marrying a despised outcaste. The story probably looks back to a much earlier time, when social relations were very much freer."[1]

But perhaps some thought should be given to whether modern scholarship, in its preoccupation with texts of a certain kind, may have lost sight of the larger social reality of the Hindu world, in which women may have exercised what are called their rights more freely than the society is given credit for. In any case, the account runs as follows:

To the beat of the drum the thief was led
to the place of execution,
and the merchant's daughter Ratnāvatī
sat on the terrace and watched him.
He was gravely wounded and covered with dust,
but as soon as she saw him she was smitten with love.
Then she went to her father Ratnadatta, and said:
"This man they are leading to his death
I have chosen for my lord!
Father, you must save him from the king,
or I will die with him!"
And when he heard, her father said:
"What is this you say, my child?
You've refused the finest suitors,
the images of the Love-god!
How can you now desire
a wretched master-thief?"
But though he reproached her thus
she was firm in her resolve,
so he sped to the king and begged
that the thief might be saved from the stake.
In return he offered
the whole of his great fortune,
but the king would not yield the thief
for ten million pieces of gold,
for he had robbed the whole city,
and was brought to the stake to repay with his life.
Her father came home in despair,
and the merchant's daughter
determined to follow
the thief in his death.
Though her family tried to restrain her
she bathed,
and mounted a litter, and went

to the place of impalement,
while her father, her mother and her people
followed her weeping.
The executioners placed
the thief on the stake,
and, as his life ebbed away,
he saw her come with her people.
He heard the onlookers speaking
of all that had happened,
For a moment he wept, and then,
smiling a little, he died.
At her order they lifted the corpse
from the stake, and took it away,
and with it the worthy merchant's daughter
mounted the pyre.[2]

Chapter 10

Animal Rights and Hinduism

Human beings are also animals from one point of view, so it was only a matter of time before the discourse on human rights would lead to the questions of animal rights. But once the issue of animal rights is raised, several questions, such as the following, arise: "When we talk about animal rights, what exactly do we mean? Do we mean that animals themselves have rights, such as not to be tortured? Or do we mean that human beings have the right not to experience the torturing of animals? Whose right is it? And does it really matter?"[1]

These are complex questions, and Dershowitz tries to answer them. From the point of Hinduism, however, a key distinction between the Western and Indic attitudes to animals becomes involved in this issue. According to the standard Western view, animals do not possess souls, but humans do. So the two do not form part of the same continuum in Western thought. The situation is different in the case of religions of Indian origin. As A. L. Basham notes:

> Together with Buddhism and Jainism, which bear to Hinduism somewhat the same relationship as Christianity and Islam bear to Judaism, Hinduism is sharply distinguished from the religions of the West by its belief in transmigration; the great religions of the world may broadly be divided into two main groups by this criterion, and Hinduism is the oldest and most enduring of the Eastern group, which maintains that the soul inhabits many bodies in its journey through the cosmos, until it reaches its final goal, which is described in varying terms by different sects. The corollary of this doctrine is that all life, whether supernatural, human, animal, insect, or with some sects even plant, is governed by the same law. Whereas Western religions

> generally teach that man is a special creation, possessing an immortal soul, which is denied to the lower animals, Hinduism maintains that all living things have souls, which are essentially equal, and are only differentiated through karma, or the effect of previous deeds, which conditions the integuments of subtle and gross matter imprisoning the souls and thus leads to their successive rebirths in different types of body. This doctrine of saṁsāra has given a very distinctive character to much Hindu thought and philosophy.[2]

Such a continuum could, however, also be envisaged in Western secular thought, for the evolution of human beings from animals allows them to be placed on a similar continuum.[3]

One could argue that "once we place the worth of animal life on a continuum, everything becomes a matter of degree. There are no natural criteria for where the appropriate lines should be drawn."[4] This, however, need not necessarily be an advantage, for moral criteria may come in play in the absence of natural criteria. We know, for instance, that rights were first claimed by an elite male class, but it was part of the human continuum, if we may put it that way, to which women and the lower classes belonged, and one way in which rights became the common property of all citizens was by their gradual devolution. Rights started out as privileges of special groups, but then these privileges were extended to other segments of the population, until they became the common property of all humans and thus became human rights.

This process of the expansion of rights has now begun to take animals within its ambit as well. Hence the issue of animal rights.[5]

The germinal idea of animal rights may be traced in ancient India to the rights that the animals enjoyed within the precincts of a hermitage. The following incident from the First Act of probably the best-known Sanskrit play in the West, the *Abhijñāna-Śākuntalam* of Kālidāsa, although somewhat prosaic in itself, takes on new life in the context of animal rights as providing an ancient Indian anticipation of it.[6]

Abhijñāna-Śākuntalam Act I

(The king enters, along with the charioteer, bow and arrow in hand, chasing a deer.)

Charioteer:	(casting a glance at the king and the deer) Sir, As I look at the deer and at you, ready to discharge an arrow, It seems I behold Śiva himself in pursuit of the deer.
King:	We have been drawn afar by this deer. Yet even now:

It looks back again and again at the chasing chariot with his neck curved gracefully. Out of fear of being hit by the arrow, it has squeezed the back of his body into the front. It scatters half-chewn grass, which has fallen from his mouth, open with exhaustion. Behold, on account of his mighty bounds, he seems to move in the sky rather than on the earth.

(With surprise) How come he can hardly be seen although I have been chasing after him?

Charioteer: Sir, I had reduced the speed of the chariot by restraining the reins, on account of the uneven nature of the terrain. Therefore the deer has moved far away. Now that we are on even ground, he will not be hard to reach.

King: Then loosen the reins.

Charioteer: As you command, Sir (mimicking the speed of the chariot).

The steeds have stretched out their bodies with the reins loosened. The tips of their fly-wisks are motionless, their ears perked-up, they are outpacing even the dust raised by them, as they vie the deers in running.

King: Indeed, they surpass the steeds of the Sun-god and of Indra. For:

That which was minute suddenly gets magnified. That which
is naturally apart seems as if linked. That which is naturally
curved, appears straight to the eye. On account of the speed
of the chariot, nothing can be said to be far or near.

Charioteer! Behold as I dispatch the deer. (Takes aim)

(Voice from behind the curtain) O King! This deer belongs to the hermitage and is not meant to be killed.

Charioteer: (hearing and then looking) Sir, the sages have come in the path of your arrow.

King: (hastily) Then restrain the horses.

Charioteer: Done. (Stops the chariot.)

(Then enters an anchorite with two others)

Anchorite: (raising his hand) King! This deer belongs to the hermitage. It should not be killed.

Do not shoot an arrow into the tender body of the deer. It would be like shooting fire into a heap of flowers. How fickle is the life of these deers and how hard and sharp your arrows. Please withdraw the arrow you have aimed so well. Your weapons are meant to protect those in distress and not to strike down the innocent.

King: Here, it is withdrawn. (Acts accordingly).

Anchorite: This is worthy of you, the shining light of the royal family of Purus.

It is meet that one born in the family of the Puru kings should act in this way. May you obtain a son possessing similar qualities who will rule over the whole world.

King: (with folded hands) I gratefully accept the benediction.[7]

Perhaps it is natural for the discussion of human rights to segue into a discussion of animal rights. When this point is discussed in relation to Indic religions, it is often pointed out, as mentioned earlier, that in Hinduism and Jainism animals possess souls—something denied to them in the Abrahamic religions. Similarly, although Buddhism does not postulate a soul and speaks of sentient beings, both humans and animals are included in this category. The implication seems to be that it is perhaps easier to make a transition from human rights into animal rights in the Indic traditions than in the Western religious traditions, which divide off human beings sharply from animals. However, inasmuch as human rights discourse is largely secular in its orientation, this aspect of Abrahamic religions may not pose an insuperable barrier to extending human rights discourse to animals.

The way these rights were extended in the Indic tradition represents an interesting development. The incipient recognition of animal rights may be traced to Buddhism's critique of Vedic animal sacrifices, sacrifices that, ultimately, went out of vogue. This tendency was perhaps reinforced by the emphasis of vegetarianism, which characterizes Jainism. It could thus be argued that, in this sense, it was the Buddhist and Jaina advocacy of animal rights that left its mark on Hinduism, a development to which the sanctity that came to be attached to the cow within Hinduism may have also contributed.

Chapter 11

Do Hindu Women Possess the Right to Study the Vedas?

Modern human rights discourse accepts that men and women are equally entitled to all forms of education. The position within Hinduism on this point is somewhat different. In the classical formulation of Hinduism, Hindu women, by and large, do not have the right to study the Vedas. There is also a strong strand of opinion within Hinduism in general that upholds this view and has the backing of scholars such as Śaṅkara (c. eighth century). At the same time, there is considerable evidence that another school of thought within Hinduism was in favor of women enjoying this right.

Bhavabhūti, the famous dramatist of the eighth century, who is rated as second only to Kālidāsa (if that), seems by *implication* to accept the view that women could study Vedānta. The figure of Ātreyī in his famous play, the *Uttararāmacarita*, leaves one in little doubt on this score, because she is specifically described as entering the Daṇḍaka forest to study Vedānta.

The right to education on the part of all is recognized in Article 26 of the Universal Declaration of Human Rights.[1] Although the context seems to imply secular knowledge, there can be little doubt that the spirit of human rights discourse requires that all forms of education, religious or secular, be equally accessible to men and women alike.

Uttararāmacarita Act II

(From behind the curtain)

Welcome to the ascetic.

(Then enters a female ascetic dressed for travel.)

Female ascetic: O, the Goddess of the Woods welcomes me from afar, with an offering of leaves containing fruits and flowers.

Enter Goddess of the Woods. (After spreading out the offering):

One can enjoy oneself as much as one likes in this forest. This is my lucky day. Virtuous people somehow come together as a result of pious deeds. We have the shade of trees, water, and food fit for ascetics, such as roots and fruits. But we don't have to rely on others.

Female ascetic: So it is said.

Friendly disposition, sweet modesty, restraint in speech, a naturally benevolent mind, blameless familiarity, an affection that does not alter with the passage of time: May this guileless secret of holy conduct prevail forever.

(The two sit down.)

Goddess of the Woods: Whom should I take you to be?

Female ascetic: I am Ātreyī.

Goddess of the Woods: Noble Ātreyī, where are you coming from and why have you come to this forest called Daṇḍaka?

Ātreyī: In this neck of the woods many reciters of the Vedas live, Agastya prominent among them. *I wish to learn Vedānta from them; therefore, I have come here,* having left Vālmīki.

Goddess of the Woods: But even other sages approach Sage Vālmīki himself, a scholar of Vedānta and the Purāṇas, for studying Vedānta, so why have you undertaken this long journey?

Ātreyī: There exists a great obstacle to pursuing studies there; therefore, I have undertaken this long journey.

Goddess of the Woods: Such as what?

Ātreyī: Some divinity brought to the sage a pair of sons who had just been weaned. They are wonderful in every way. They warm the cockles of the heart of not only the sages but all living beings.

Goddess of the Woods: Do they have a name?

Ātreyī: That very divinity told us their names were Kuśa and Lava and also about their prowess.

Goddess of the Woods: What prowess?

Ātreyī: They know how to use the secret divine weapons from the moment they were born.

Goddess of the Woods: This is most unusual.

Ātreyī: Those two were raised by Sage Vālmīki, acting as their wet nurse. After their tonsure ceremony had been performed, they were carefully made to master the three sciences, other than the three Vedas. Thereafter, when they turned eleven, they were initiated into Vedic studies by their Guru Vālmīki and taught the three Vedas. *It is not possible for people like me to study with them, as they far outshine us in intelligence and memory.* For:

> The teacher instructs both the bright and the dull student equally and does not either add to or take away anything from their comprehension. But a great difference is found in the result. A pure jewel is able to reflect (other objects), but not a lump of clay.[2]

The fact that Bhavabhūti chose to depict a woman, by the name of Ātreyī, as engaged in the pursuit of Vedantic studies may not be an accident. On the contrary, it might signify a deep familiarity with Hindu lore. As is well known, some of the hymns of the ṚgVeda are attributed by the Hindu religious tradition itself to women seers, although modern scholarship tends to be skeptical in the matter. It is nevertheless the case that the *Sarvānukramaṇikā* lists "as many as twenty women among the 'seers' or authors of the ṚgVeda."[3] Although some of these names, such as those of Indrāṇī and Śacī, sound mythical, scholars tend to be more accepting of the ascription of V.28 to Viśvavārā; VIII.91 to Apālā and X.39 to Ghoṣā Kākṣīvatī.[4] What is noteworthy from our point of view is the fact that Viśvavārā and Apālā belong to the family of Atri.[5] This association of women of the Atri family with the seers of the ṚgVeda is confirmed by *Jaiminīya Brāhmaṇa* (II.219), which states that women of the Ātreya clan were *mantra*-makers: *striyo mantrakrta āsuḥ*.[6]

Further evidence that women participated in discussions of Vedānta is provided by the examples of Maitreyī and Gārgī. One could, however, argue that these were exceptional cases. Evidence of the fact that female participation in Vedānta was more broadbased is provided by some manuscripts of the *Aitareya Upaniṣad.* In ten out of thirty-eight manuscripts noted by A. B. Keith,[7] one finds the readings: *apakrāmantu garbhiṇyaḥ* and *yathāsthānam tu garbhiṇyaḥ* at the beginning and end of the second chapter, respectively.[8] The first statement asks pregnant women in the audience to leave, and the second asks them to resume their place. This variant reading is documented by Keith and duly noted by Patrick Olivelle but is not referred to by either Hume[9] or Radhakrishnan.[10] Many Hindi editions of the text include the reading. The two entries pertaining to the absence and presence of pregnant women thus seem to constitute a credible, if not a universal, textual tradition. A. B. Keith however remarks: "But though old the words cannot be original and are not recognized by Sāyaṇa or Śaṅkara."[11] This, however, seems to be a classic case of begging the question. Both Sāyaṇa and Śaṅkara belong to a period when women were no longer formally admitted to Vedic studies, so the fact that they do not recognize it cannot perhaps carry much independent authority. These variants seem to confirm the participation of women in general in such studies in the *Upanisadic* milieu. This last point is hardly new, given the roles played by Gārgī and Maitreyī in the *Bṛhadāraṇyaka Upaniṣad* (III:6,8; II:4; IV.5). It could be argued, however, that, even though Gārgī might have been a *brahmacāriṇī*, Maitreyī was married. She was, however, apparently not pregnant when Yājñavalkya delivered his famous farewell address to her. This new variant reading enables us to go beyond this and state with confidence that *pregnant women* participated in the *Upaniṣadic* sessions (until the subject matter under consideration became somewhat delicate, in view of their condition). One has come a long way from initially wondering whether women participated in *Upaniṣadic* gatherings, to the point of being able to claim that not only a few women, known by their names, did so, but that women in general did so, and pregnant women at that. The significance of the variant reading consists in providing the evidence for enabling such a claim to be made.

Chapter 12

The Rights of the Child and the Right to Parenthood: A Case Study

Modern Western discourse on human rights is fully committed to the rights of the child, a process that culminated in the proclamation of the Convention on the Rights of the Child in 1989. Its preamble is worth citing, because it virtually recapitulates the history of the rights of the child in current human rights discourse.

Convention on the Rights of the Child

Preamble

The States Parties to the present Convention,

Considering that, in accordance with the principles proclaimed in the Charter of the United Nations, recognition of the inherent dignity and of the equal and inalienable rights of all members of the human family is the foundation of freedom, justice and peace in the world,

Bearing in mind that the peoples of the United Nations have, in the Charter, reaffirmed their faith in fundamental human rights and in the dignity and worth of the human person, and have determined to promote social progress and better standards of life in larger freedom,

Recognizing that the United Nations has, in the Universal Declaration of Human Rights and in the International Covenants on Human Rights, proclaimed and agreed that everyone is entitled to all the rights and freedoms set forth therein, without distinction of any kind, such as race, colour, sex, language, religion, political or other opinion, national or social origin, property, birth or other status,

Recalling that, in the Universal Declaration of Human Rights, the United Nations has proclaimed that childhood is entitled to special care and assistance,

Convinced that the family, as the fundamental group of society and the natural environment for the growth and well-being of all its members and particularly children, should be afforded the necessary protection and assistance so that it can fully assume its responsibilities within the community.

Recognizing that the child, for the full and harmonious development of his or her personality, should grow up in a family environment, in an atmosphere of happiness, love and understanding,

Considering that the child should be fully prepared to live an individual life in society, and brought up in the spirit of the ideals proclaimed in the Charter of the United Nations, and in particular in the spirit of peace, dignity, tolerance, freedom, equality and solidarity,

Bearing in mind that the need to extend particular care to the child has been stated in the Geneva Declaration of the Rights of the Child of 1924 and in the Declaration of the Rights of the Child adopted by the General Assembly on 20 November 1959 and recognized in the Universal Declaration of Human Rights, in the International Covenant on Civil and Political Rights (in particular in Articles 23 and 24), in the International Covenant on Economic, Social and Cultural Rights (in particular in Article 10) and in the statutes and relevant instruments of specialized agencies and international organizations concerned with the welfare of children,

Bearing in mind that, as indicated in the Declaration of the Rights of the Child, "the child, by reasons of his physical and mental immaturity, needs special safeguards and care, including appropriate legal protection, before as well as after birth,"

Recalling the provisions of the Declaration on Social and Legal Principles relating to the Protection and Welfare of Children, with Special Reference to Foster Placement and Adoption Nationally and Internationally; the United Nations Standard Minimum Rules for the Administration of Juvenile Justice (The Beijing Rules); and the Declaration on the Protection of Women and Children in Emergency and Armed Conflict,

Recognizing that, in all countries in the world, there are children living in exceptionally difficult conditions, and that such children need special consideration,

Taking due account of the importance of the traditions and cultural values of each people for the protection and harmonious development of the child,

Recognizing the importance of international co-operation fro improving the living conditions of children in every country, in particular in the developing countries,

Have agreed as follows . . . [1]

With this in the background, it is worth reproducing the first three articles of the Convention to place the significance of the Hindu narrative in the proper context. These articles run as follows:

Article 1
For the purposes of the present Convention, a child means every human being below the age of eighteen years unless, under the law applicable to the child, majority is attained earlier.

Article 2
1. States Parties shall respect and ensure the rights set forth in the present Convention to each child within their jurisdiction without discrimination of any kind, irrespective of the child's or his or her parent's or legal guardian's race, colour, sex, language, religion, political or other opinion, national, ethnic or social origin, property, disability, birth or other status.
2. States Parties shall take all appropriate measures to ensure that the child is protected against all forms of discrimination or punishment on the basis of the status, activities, expressed opinions, or beliefs of the child's parents, legal guardians, or family members.

Article 3
1. In all actions concerning children, whether undertaken by public or private social welfare institutions, courts of law, administrative authorities or legislative bodies, the best interests of the child shall be a primary consideration.
2. States Parties undertake to ensure the child such protection and care as is necessary for his or her well-being, taking into account the rights and duties of his or her parents, legal guardians, or other individuals legally responsible for him or her, and, to this end, shall take all appropriate legislative and administrative measure.
3. States parties shall ensure that the institutions, services and facilities responsible for the care or protection of children shall conform with the standards established by competent authorities, particularly in the areas of safety, health, in the number and suitability of their staff, as well as competent supervision.[2]

It is worth noting in the context of these Articles that Clause 2 of Article 3 states: "States parties undertake to assure the child for his or her well-being, taking into account the rights and duties *of his or her parents*."[3] The concept of parenthood is accepted here as something quite self-evident. The Hindu narrative problematizes this concept.

A locution such as the *right to parenthood* must sound odd to begin with. One might have heard of the rights of children and of parents' rights (especially in relation to children), but not of the right to parenthood. The locution, however, is stranger than the situation it represents, which is regularly encountered, as in the case of the state appointing itself as the ward of children not adequately cared for by the parents. In such cases the biological right to parenthood yields to the ideological right to parenthood, when its social expectations are not fulfilled.

The narrative that follows raises the question: Who is a father? Thus it helps problematize the question of parenthood from the perspective of human rights discourse. This very old story may help us think our way through some very modern human rights predicaments.

The story begins, as many such stories do, with a childless royal couple. Hariścandra, the famed king of Banaras, and his queen, Candramatī, were childless. Under the advice of their royal chaplain, Vasiṣṭha, they decided to perform penance in honor of god Varuṇa on the banks of the Ganges. Viśvāmitra, a rival of Vasiṣṭha for priestly honors, did not approve of this.

God Varuṇa, pleased by the penance, appeared before Hariścandra and promised him a son. Hariścandra, somewhat like Abraham, promised to sacrifice the son in honor of Varuṇa, should the wish be fulfilled.

The wish was fulfilled. Candramatī conceived and in good time was delivered of a son, who was named Rohitāśva. Once the son was born, however, Hariścandra was reluctant to offer him in sacrifice to Varuṇa and tarried. Varuṇa nevertheless kept demanding that the king keep his word. It was then settled that the son would be offered to the god after he had turned eleven and had been invested with the sacred thread.

When the boy reached the right age and preparations were under way for the investiture ceremony, Varuṇa arrived at the palace and demanded the son. The son, in the meantime, came to know of his imminent sacrifice and fled to the forest from the palace. God Varuṇa, enraged at these developments, cursed the king with dropsy, and the king became a sick man. The truant boy, in the meantime, heard of his father's condition and wanted to see him but was dissuaded by the god Indra, in the form of a Brahmin, from doing so.

The afflicted king sought advice from his chaplain, Vasiṣṭha. The chaplain advised that there are ten types of sons, a classification that includes a son who has been purchased. He therefore advised the king to purchase a son and offer it to Varuṇa in place of Rohitāśva. The king liked the idea and instructed his ministers accordingly. They found a Brahmin, Ajīgarta by name, willing to sell his son, Śunaḥśepa, for a hundred cows. The deal was struck.

Viśvāmitra, the rival of Vasiṣṭha, was following these developments. When Śunaḥśepa, the substitute son who had been purchased for a consideration, was brought to the palace, he was approached by

Viśvāmitra. The child was crying piteously. Viśvāmitra asked the king to release the boy and threatened to disrupt the sacrifice in which Śunaḥśepa was to be offered to Varuṇa. The king urged him not to do so, because he wanted to regain his health, and offered Viśvāmitra financial inducements to desist from his course. This made Viśvāmitra all the more determined to intervene. He took Śunaḥśepa aside, taught him the Varuṇamantra (a hymn in praise of Varuṇa), and instructed him to recite it when he was laid down for slaughter on the slab.

Śunaḥśepa did as he was told and, at the critical moment, invoked Varuṇa. Varuṇa thereupon appeared in person, had Śunaḥśepa released, and cured the king with his blessing. Then he disappeared.

It is at this point that the story becomes one of interest from the perspective of human rights. Śunaḥśepa's escape from death posed a key question. Who was his *father by right now*?

Opinions were divided on the issue. Some said that Ajīgarta was still his father, others insisted that his father was Hariścandra, and still others maintained that Varuṇa, who had spared his life, was now his father. At this point Vasiṣṭha offered the following magnanimous resolution to the dilemma. He argued that the biological father, Ajīgarta, lost all right to paternity when he sold his son, knowing full well what awaited him. Hariścandra, his commercial father, as it were, after purchasing him, also lost all right to the son's paternity when he had him tied for slaughter. As for Varuṇa, it is true that the god saved Śunaḥśepa's life, but this is what gods are supposed to do when they are invoked and praised.

He therefore ruled that Viśvāmitra, who had taught Śunaḥśepa the Varuṇa-mantra, was henceforth his father.

The story ends on a happy note. The king recovered from his illness, whereupon Rohitāśva came out of the forest and joined his father in the palace. Viśvāmitra took Śunaḥśepa along with him to his hermitage, and the king, the wife, and his son lived happily ever after.[4]

Strange as it may sound, it is also possible to problematize "motherhood," a possibility that bordered on the ludicrous a decade ago but has now been brought in the realm of the possible by in-vitro fertilization. The Hindu account of the birth of Kārtikeya is relevant here.

The gods and the demons were once again at odds, and the demons had once again pushed the gods into a corner. The beleaguered gods approached God for advice and were told that the demons would be defeated if the armies of the gods were led by the son of Śiva.

This stipulation presented a problem, because Śiva was at the time a celibate practicing austerities, although Pārvatī had fallen in love with him and wanted to marry him.

The gods urged Kāma—the Indian Cupid—to display his skill, but, as soon as Śiva sensed his presence, he zapped the god of love to ashes. Kāma's discomfiture carried an important lesson for Pārvatī—she could not hope to win Śiva over by her feminine beauty and charm any longer.

But Pārvatī was not about to give up and embarked on a course of austerities that brought her to the notice of Śiva, who was duly impressed. This is how the marriage of Śiva and Pārvatī came about.

The consummation of the marriage, however, brought fresh problems. Śiva and Pārvatī began to make love, but days passed into nights. Even ages passed, and the gods became afraid that the product of so unceasing a begetting might be too much for the universe to bear. They urged Śiva to desist from his conjugal exertions, but the question arose as to what was to be done with the seed already stored up. The god Agni offered to bear it.

> Fire (Agni) was made to receive Śiva's burning seed. Unable to endure its heat, Agni threw it into the river Ganges. The mighty river goddess Gaṅgā, unable to carry its consuming heat, deposited the fetus in the mountains, in a grove of reeds. There a child was born. The Pleiades (Kṛttikās) nursed the infant; they were its foster mothers. Named after the Kṛttikās, Kārttikeya was to be the commander of the army of the gods in their war against the demons. Some considered Gaṅgā, who had carried the fetus, to be Kārttikeya's mother[5]

Once again, we have to answer the question: "Who was Kārtikeya's mother?"—just as we had to ask who was Śunaḥśepa's father, and once again there are three candidates: Pārvatī, Gaṅgā, and the Kṛttikās.

It is only a question of time before human rights discourse comes face to face with such problems and the rights of parents, like the rights of children, emerge as a category within it.

Chapter 13

A Discussion of Law and Morality from Ancient India

The ensuing section is excerpted from the *Mahābhārata*. The reader will note how two dialogues are emboxed within it—a typical narrative feature of the epic. The question is put by Yudhiṣṭhira to Bhīṣma, and Bhīṣma answers it by reproducing a dialogue between Dyumatsena and Satyavān. These two characters appear earlier in the narrative of Sāvitrī, wherein Dyumatsena is her father-in-law and Satyavān her husband. Dyumatsena himself says what he does by recalling a conversation he had earlier, with a pious *brāhmaṇa.*

This part of the *Mahābhārata* has attracted attention because it questions capital punishment and introduces other interesting themes. It can also be looked upon as a dialogue between an idealist (Satyavān) and a realist (Dyumatsena). P. V. Kane offers an interesting summary of the dialogue, which might serve to introduce it:

> The Śāntiparva chap. 268 [Critical Edition Chap. 259] contains an interesting dialogue between king Dyumatsena and his son prince Satyavat on the subject of the punishment of death, which contains some of the arguments forcibly urged in these days by those that are opposed to capital punishment altogether. The prince pleads that punishment should be light even for grave offences, that when the sentence of death is carried out in the case of robbers, several innocent persons (such as the wife, the mother, the son of the condemned man) suffer great loss (and they may die also), that if offenders give themselves up to priests, swear before them that they will never commit sin, they may be let off after undergoing penance, that if great men go astray their punishment should be proportionate to their greatness. The king replies that in former ages when people were most truthful, soft-hearted, and not hot-tempered the punishment of saying "fie

on you" sufficed; then vocal remonstrances and upbraidings sufficed, but in the later ages (of Kali) corporal punishment and death sentence have to be resorted to and that some people are not deterred even by the fear of death sentence.[1]

Yudhiṣṭhira said: How might a ruler protect the subjects without oppressing them? O best of saints, this is my question to you. Please answer it.

Bhīṣma said: In this matter an ancient account is alluded to in the form of a dialogue between Dyumatsena and king Satyavān.

We have heard that Satyvān said something unprecedented when he saw people being taken for execution by the order of his father:

"It is true that something what is apparently moral may not be really so and what is apparently immoral may really turn out to be the moral course of action. But it is not possible that killing people could ever be considered moral."

Dyumatsena said: What would you call moral if killing the felons is considered immoral? If the malcontents are not killed, O Satyavān, it will lead to chaos.

In Kali Yuga people will claim as theirs what is not theirs, and it will be virtually impossible to lead a normal life. But if you would rather follow some other course of action, then let me know what it is.

Satyavān said: All the three *varṇas* should be placed in charge of the *brāhmaṇas*. When they are bound to proper moral conduct, there will be little deviation.

Whosoever misbehaves among them will be reported to the king by the *brāhmaṇa* as follows: "He does not listen to me." The king will then punish him.

One should implement that law which does not lead to loss of life. One should not cause loss of life without properly examining the actual actions and moral precepts.

The king takes the life of felons and of many innocent people as well, but when they are killed, so are their wife, mother, father, and son. Therefore the king should punish with great care because it involves harming others.

Sometimes a bad person turns a new leaf, and good people also produce bad children.

It could not possibly be the immemorial tradition that one should strike at the root. It should be possible to make someone pay for a crime without killing being involved.

The guilty could be threatened, or bound, or disfigured. They should not be tormented by death or grievous injury.

When they seek refuge with a priest and take the oath: "Priest, we will not do so again"—then they should be set free. Such should be the rule of law (or of the king). [On the other hand] even a *brāhmaṇa* who is clean-shaven and carries a staff and antelope skin deserves to be detained.

The highest penalty should be inflicted in the case of habitual offenders, but not in the case of a first offense.

Dyumatsena said: That arrangement should be considered consistent with *dharma,* by which all the subjects can be kept in control wherever they are, so long as it is not violated.

If those who are to be killed are not killed, then everything will be lost. In the most ancient times people were easy to govern.

They were pliant, mostly honest, and just a little bit rebellious and violent. In ancient times the only punishment was condemnation; thereafter rebuke had to be administered.

Then came fine also and seizure of property, and now death-penalty is also enforced. But now people can't be kept in check even through capital punishment.

With a felon, it is said, no one counts for anything, whether one be human, or divine, or semi-divine, or an ancestor.

They will loot even the clothes of the dead from the cremation-ground and even the wealth of the gods. How is one to deal with these mindless ignorant ones?

Satyavān said: If you are unable to protect the innocent (without resorting to killing, or are unable to save the felons by converting them into virtuous people through nonviolence), then some way of compensating them in the past, present, and future should be figured out.

Dyumatsena said: The rulers go to great lengths to ensure that people lead normal lives. They are ashamed of the criminals and therefore act in such a (draconian) manner.

People behave themselves through fear of the law; (the rulers) do not kill the criminal because they enjoy doing so. By and large the rulers govern their subjects benevolently.

In this way the people follow the best possible course of action. Human beings always emulate the behavior of their superiors.

One who instructs others in how they might be at peace, without being at peace himself, while indulging in luxurious living—such a person is scoffed at by the people.

If anyone acts in an improper way toward a ruler out of hypocrisy or delusion, then he should be brought to book in every possible way. In this way he gives up acting in an evil manner.

One who wants to bring evil under control should begin by bringing himself under control. He should impose the highest penalty on his closest relatives.

Crime flourishes where a convicted criminal is not punished severely and moral standards collapse. This is how I was instructed by the learned compassionate *brāhmaṇa*.

[He also told me] my dear, this is how I was myself well instructed by my compassionate grandsires as a favor.

In Kṛtayuga, the king ruled by the excellent method (of *ahiṁsā*). With the coming of Tretāyuga, the ruler governed with *dharma* reduced by a quarter; in the Dvāpara, reduced by two quarters, and by another quarter in the next.

So with the onset of Kaliyuga, only a sixteenth part of *dharma* is left, on account of the misdemeanor of kings and the nature of the age.

O, Satyavān, if one followed that excellent method (of *ahiṁsā*) chaos will ensue (in the Kali age). In this age one should order punishment, keeping the age, capacity, and occasion in mind.

Manu proclaimed the law for the well-being of all creatures so that they may not lose the fruit of *dharma*, which is leads to Truth.

Mahābhārata 12.259.1-35

Chapter 14

Hinduism and Egalitarianism

One special feature of human rights discourse is the fact that these rights belong to all human beings *without exception*. Viewed from such a perspective, "the rights revolution is a story of inclusion, of how previously excluded groups obtained rights of equality."[1]

Hinduism, on the other hand, has been associated with the concept of caste, which divides society up into unequal classes. This had led scholars to propose that the application of human rights concepts to Hinduism poses special problems. Thus Klaus K. Klostermaier remarks that "basically, the Brahmins did not develop 'human rights' but 'caste rights' which had the side effect that in the course of time about one-fifth of the total population, as 'outcastes' had virtually no rights."[2]

One would therefore like to provide an example of the enormity of the challenge human rights discourse poses to Hinduism. The point is illustrated in the following incident from the *Rāmāyaṇa*, which is the *bête noire* of Indian liberals, and justly so, because it depicts Rāma, an ideal king according to Hindu mythology, putting a low-caste person to death for practicing austerities reserved only for the higher castes. The incident is found in the *Uttara-kāṇḍa* of the *Rāmāyaṇa*:

After a few days had passed, an old Brahmin from the countryside approached the royal gate, carrying the dead body of a child in his arms.

Crying out for his child in many ways with words of love, he kept saying again and again: "O my child, O my child!

What sin did I commit in my previous incarnation as a result of which I live to see the death of my only son?

My son had not even seen youth, he was only five years old and died an untimely death to my utter grief.

I will doubtless die in a few days myself and so will your mother, O son, out of grief at your death.

I do not recall ever uttering a lie or killing someone, then on what account has my son, while still a child, been taken to death's door before he could perform the rites to the ancestors.

I have neither seen or heard such a terrible thing—this occurrence of a premature death in the land of Rāma.

Without doubt some great sin of Rāma himself is involved in this. You, King! must revive my dead child.

O King, may you attain to long life along with your brothers. O mighty one, we were dwelling happily in your kingdom.

But now the land is no longer under the protection of Ikṣvāku kings, now that we have a king in Rāma who is to be held responsible for the death of a child.

Disasters befall subjects, who have not been properly governed, on account of the faults of the king. A person dies prematurely when the king's conduct is impious.

The fear of premature death arises when no protection is afforded against the evil deeds committed by people in the cities and the villages.

Both in the city and the village this death of the child will be clearly attributed to the fault of the kings."

Talking in this way and censuring the king repeatedly, he clung to his son, beside himself with grief.

King Rāma heard, to the very end, the piteous and grief-stricken lamentation of that Brahmin.

He, feeling deeply hurt, summoned his councilors, brothers, civic leaders, Vaśiṣtha and Vāmadeva.

Then Vasiṣṭha ushered in eight Brahmins in the presence of the king, who shone forth like a god. They then blessed him—"Prosper."

They were Mārkaṇḍeya, Maudgalya, Vāmadeva, Kāśyapa, Kātyāyana, Jābāli, Gautama, and Nārada.

These foremost among the Brahmins were given a seat, and so also the councilors and civil leaders as per protocol.

After all of them, shining in their splendor, had been seated, Rāma told them all about why the Brahmin was crying.

Nārada then spoke these auspicious words in the presence of the sages, upon hearing the words of the distressed king.

"O king! Listen to why the child has died prematurely and then, O brave descendant of Raghu, do what needs to be done.

O Rāma, formerly in the Kṛta Yuga only Brahmins practiced asceticism. O king, none who was not a Brahmin was an ascetic then.

When that glorious, Brahmanic age came to be, everyone born in it was endowed with immortality and possessed divine vision.

Then indeed followed Tretāyuga, when the sons of Manu acquire a body and *kṣatriyas* are born, imbued with austerities performed earlier on.

Those sons of Manu, who excelled in a previous life on account of their power and austerity; those great souled ones were born in that Tretāyuga.

In both these ages, all the Brahmins and the Kṣatriyas were on par without any distinction.

Then all of them established the Fourfold Order everywhere, as things developed further.

Adharma had by now placed one step on the earth; the Twice-Borns, upon coming in touch with *adharma,* lost their luster.

Then the life-spans became limited, but the people behaved well, being devoted to truth and virtue.

All those who were Brāhmaṇas and Kṣatriyas in the course of Tretāyuga practiced austerities, and the rest were devoted to serving them.

That came to be the supreme duty of the Vaiśyas and the Śūdras. And the Śūdras were especially devoted to serving all the classes.

Then the second foot of *adharma* fell. That age came to be recokened as Dvāparayuga.

When the Dvāpara age came to pass, as the *yugas* declined, then, O best of men, *adharma* and falsehood increased.

In the Dvāparayuga, the practice of austerity spread among the Vaiśyas. O king, but a *śūdra* could not undertake the course of fierce austerities.

However, O king, in the Kaliyuga, a person of an inferior *varṇa* will perform great austerities. Austerity will be practiced by those born *śūdras.*

O Rāma, in the Dvāparayuga the practice of austerity by a *śūdra* is an act of supreme *adharma.* O king, in your borderland austerities are being performed by a great but perverse *śūdra.* The child has died because of that.

Whosoever foolish man performs an act that should not be performed, O best of kings, in either the country or the city, soon doubtless goes to hell and so also the king.

So, O best of kings, you should scour your land, and, wherever you see a sin being committed, put it down swiftly.

O best of kings, this will increase the piety and the life-span of the people and restore the child's life."

Upon hearing those words of Nārada, which were like nectar, Rāma was pleased beyond measure and spoke as follows to Lakṣmaṇa.

"O gentle Lakṣmaṇa, go and console the best of Brāhmins. Place the body of the child in a vat of oil.

O gentle one, apply the best perfumes and most fragrant oils, so that the child's body does not decompose.

See to it that the body of the innocent and sheltered child does not split open or is harmed in any way."

Rāma thus directed Lakṣmaṇa, who was auspicious to look at, and the celebrated Rāma then summoned Puṣpaka in the mind.

Puṣpaka, adorned with gold, read the signal and arrived by Rāma's side in a moment.

He bowed and said, "King! Here I am. O one with long arms—I am at your command ready to do your bidding."

The king heard the pleasant words of Puṣpaka and mounted the plane after saluting the sages.

He placed the two, Lakṣmaṇa and Bharata, in charge of the city, and grabbing his bow, quiver and shining scimitar, went west to Meru searching everywhere. Then he turned in the northern direction bounded by the Himalayas.

Even there he saw no signs of evil-doing; the king then also explored the whole eastern region.

Then the favorite of the royal seers turned south and saw a huge lake by the side of the Śaivāla Mountain.

King Rāma saw an ascetic performing sever austerities suspended in the air, with his face downward on the banks of the lake.

He then approached this ascetic, who was performing this wonderful penance. Then Rāma spoke to him as follows: "You are to be congratulated, O follower of excellent vows!

O ascetic! In which caste were your born? O firm of vows! I Rāma, son of Dāśaratha, would like to know.

I want to know, ascetic, what you wish to gain—heaven or a boon, by undertaking this course of austerity.

O pious one! O invincible one! Are you a *brāhmaṇa*, a *kṣatriya*, a *vaiśya,* or a *śūdra*—tell me the truth."

Upon hearing these words of virtuous Rāma, he replied to him from his position as he was, with his head hanging downward.

"I am a *śūdra* by birth and have undertaken rigorous penance with the desire, O Rāma, of entering heaven in bodily form.

O king, I am not lying, I have undertaken this penance with the aim of conquering heaven. O Rāma! I am a *śūdra,* and Śambūka is my name."

Even as the *śūdra* was talking, Rāma chopped his soft head with his stainless scimitar after drawing it from its sheath.

At that very moment the child came back to life.

Then the lotus-eyed Rāma proceeded to the hermitage of Agastya. He approached him modestly and rejoiced, brimming with happiness, after bowing to him.

After saluting that sage, who was shining as it were with brilliance, the king sat down, enjoying sumptuous hospitality.

The great sage, Agastya, great alike in luster and asceticism, said to him: "Welcome, O best of kings; O Rāma it is very fortunate that you have come.

I esteem you greatly on account of your many excellent qualities. You are an honored guest and always enjoy a place in my heart.

The gods tell me that you have arrived after killing a *śūdra* and that you have revived the dead son of a *brāhmaṇa* by resorting to *dharma*."

Rāmāyaṇa VII.64.2 to VII.67.10

Although, on the face of it, this account looks highly inimical to the concept of human rights, it bears closer examination. It depicts the state of affairs when, according to Hindu mythology, Rāma was king. This rule of Rāma in Hindu chronology is assigned to the Tretāyuga. We are currently living in the Kaliyuga, or the last of the series of four *yugas,* of which Tretāyuga is the second.

Rāma slew Śambuka, a *śūdra,* for practising austerities in Tretāyuga. Now the relevant question to ask is this: Does a *śūdra* have to be slain for practicing austerities in our age, in Kaliyuga?

To find an answer to this question, one needs to revert to the earlier portion of the account, where Nārada divines the cause of the premature death of the Brahmin's son and attributes it to a *śūdra* practicing austerities in Tretāyuga. But in the same context he also states that, in Kaliyuga, *śūdras* will possess the right to practice austerities. So the problem is solved by a change of context—what was proper in the time of Rāma is not proper now.

But there is more to it than being able to claim that the right to practice austerities has become a human right within Hinduism. The *manner* in which it has become a human right, apart from the *fact,* is equally instructive. It has become a human right with its gradual expansion through the ages. The four main ages in Hinduism are the Kṛtayuga, the Tretāyuga, the Dvāparayuga, and the Kaliyuga. The four classes or *varṇas* consist of

(1) the *brāhmaṇas*, (2) the *kṣatriyas*, (3) the *vaiśyas*, and (4) the *śūdras*. This extension of the right to practice asceticism can be depicted with the help of a chart, which correlates the two categories of *yugas* and *varṇa* as follows:

Right to Practice Austerities

Age	*Varṇa* to which the right belongs
Kṛta Yuga	*Brāhmaṇas*
Tretā Yuga	*Brāhmaṇas, Kṣatriyas*
Dvāpara Yuga	*Brāhmaṇas, Kṣatriyas, Vaiśyas*
Kali Yuga	*Brāhmaṇas, Kṣatriyas, Vaiśyas, Śūdras*

What is remarkable about this pattern is the similarity it bears to the way rights were gradually expanded in modern times—to include more and more categories of people, until they embraced the whole of humanity.

Chapter 15

Hinduism and the Rights of the Dead

There has been much talk, in the recent discourse on human rights, about the rights of the unborn and the dying. Thus both the beginning and the end of life have been problematized from the point of view of human rights, as it were. But to speak of the rights of the dead? This does strain one's credulity.

Hard as it might be to believe, this could well constitute a Hindu contribution to the discourse on human rights, even if the setting in which the issue surfaces is not entirely pleasant.

The context is provided by an incident in the *Rāmāyaṇa.* Rāvaṇa has just been killed in an earth-shaking battle by Rāma, and Rāvaṇa's wife, Mandodarī, has just shed tears over the dead body. Vibhīṣaṇa is the brother of Rāvaṇa, now dead.

Rāma then said to Vibhīṣaṇa: Please perform the last rites of your brother and make these women go back. The courteous Vibhīṣaṇa, upon hearing what Rāma had said, turned it over in his mind, and then the righteous one offered the following reply to Rāma, following up on what Rāma had said:

> "I don't feel like performing the rites for one who was cruel, heartless, a fake, who had abandoned righteous conduct, and who forced himself on the wives of others.
>
> He was up to no good and really an enemy of mine in the form of a brother. Although he should be respected on account of his seniority, Rāvaṇa does not deserve it.

People on the earth may brand my conduct as cruel, O Rāma, to begin with, but they will praise it when they come to know all the facts."

Rāma, the best among the virtuous, was much pleased by hearing these words, and then he said this to Vibhīṣaṇa, who, like him, also knew the right thing to say.

"I owe you a favor. I was victorious on your account. O king of demons, so do forgive me for saying what I must. This demon was indeed full of vice and falsehood, (but) he was also brilliant, tough and brave in battle.

I am told he could not be defeated by Indra and the gods, and he was spirited and strong, that Rāvaṇa who so distressed the people.

Enmities last only until death. Our purpose is served. Perform his rites; he was to me as you are to me.

O one with long arms, he deserves to have his last rites duly performed by you without delay. O knower of dharma—you will be acclaimed for doing that."

Then, Vibhīṣaṇa had the proper rites for Ràvaṇa performed quickly upon hearing these words of Rāma.

Vibhīṣaṇa duly lighted his pyre and made those women return, consoling them again and again. After all the female demons had gone, Vibhīṣaṇa sat down politely by Rāma's side.

Rāma with Sugrīva, Lakṣmaṇa, and the rest of the army then rejoiced on having killed the enemy, like Indra after killing Vṛtra.

Rāmāyaṇa 6.99.30-44

The previously mentioned account is found in the critical text of the *Rāmāyaṇa*. The vulgate text of the *Rāmāyaṇa* provides some additional interesting details that are not irrelevant to our discussion. These pertain to the funeral ceremony:

At these words of Raghava, Bibishana hastened to carry out the funeral rites.

Entering the city of Lanka, that Indra among the Titans, Bibishana, began to prepare for the Agnihotra Ceremony in honor of his brother. Carts, wood of varying essences, fire, utensils, sandal, logs of every kind, fragrant gums, perfumes, cloths, jewels, pearls, and coral were all assembled by him, and he soon returned surrounded by titans, whereupon, accompanied by Malyavan, he initiated the sacrifice.

Having placed Ravana, the supreme Lord of the Titans, wrapped in linen cloths on a golden bier, the Twice-Borns with bibishana at their head, their eyes suffused with tears, raised the litter decorated with many fragrant and divine symbols, to the sound of innumerable musical instruments and funeral chants, and all, turning their faces toward the south, took up pieces of wood that had been distributed among them.

Then the brahmins, versed in the Yajur Veda, bearing flaming brands went forward and those who had taken refuge with them, and the women of the inner apartments followed, sobbing with tottering steps, running hither and thither. And Ravana was placed in a spacious ground, amidst profound lamentation, and a great pyre was built with pieces of Sandal and Padmaka Wood and grass, according to tradition; and he was covered with antelope skins.

Thereafter, in honor of the King of the Titans, a rare offering was made to the ancestors, and the altar was installed to the south-west with the sacred fire in its proper place. Then curd and clarified butter were poured on Ravana's shoulder, and wooden mortar placed at his feet, with one between his thighs; vessels of wood and the lower and upper kindling sticks, with a spare pestle, were set there according to the prescribed rules. Now the titans sacrificed a goat in honor of their king, according to tradition, as taught by the great Rishis, and, having dipped a cloth in butter, they covered the face of their sovereign, who was adorned with garlands and sprinkled with perfumes. Thereafter Bibishana's companions, their faces bathed in tears, covered the body with cloths and every kind of roasted grain, whereupon Bibishana kindled the pyre according to the sacred rites, and, having laved him with a cloth that had been previously wetted with water and mingled with linseed and sacrificial grass, he bowed down to him; then he addressed the consorts of Ravana again and again in order to console them, finally entreating them to return home. And when they had all re-entered the City of Lanka, that Indra among the Titans took up his place by Rama in an attitude of reverence.

Rama, however, with his army, Sugriva, and Lakshmana, rejoiced at the death of his enemy, as the God who bears the Thunderbolt on the destruction of Vritra.[1]

It was important to provide this description of the ceremony with which Rāvaṇa was cremated, for it has a crucial bearing on the implication of the excerpted text from the *Rāmāyaṇa* for the discourse on human rights. It adds force to the issue raised by the verses that preceded it—namely, do the dead have rights too?

Because the issue seems potentially to be a narrow one, one might begin by placing it in a broader perspective, involving religion, violence, and human rights. It could be broadened further by incorporating within it elements of not only human rights but also of human dignity.

One may begin by offering two introductory remarks. The first is that, for the purposes of this discussion, one may assume that it is analytically advantageous to carry out the discussion in terms of the twin concepts of *human rights and human dignity.* Sometimes these two terms are used almost synonymously; when a distinction is drawn between the two, there is a tendency to view human dignity as the more comprehensive of the two. Both the terms shall be used in both ways—sometimes as interchangeable and sometimes as distinct, sometimes dual but undivided, and yet at other times as two separate concepts, but united, even in tension.

The second introductory remark is not unrelated to the first. As the remarks proceed, the reader will discover that the topic is being approached through a series of successively broadening circles of orientation. The question of the dignity of the dead, or those about to be killed, will be examined first. Here the issue is one of human dignity in the face of violence, or in the face of a violent end. The next concentric circle will examine the possibility of defending human dignity—not against but *through* violence. A third circle will encompass the question of maintaining the dignity of combatants and noncombatants in the course of war—that secularly ritualized enactment of violence. Finally, the largest conceptual circle in terms of Hindu and Indic civilization will be drawn, which seems to dignify violence itself at times and examine its implications.

In brief, dignity *in* violence, dignity *through* violence, dignity while *engaged* in violence and, finally, *dignifying* violence are the four themes that shall be touched upon.

Before one proceeds further, however, a few comments on the timeliness of the topic of the theme may also be offered. The word timeliness is used advisedly. It is one of the virtues whose cultivation is recommended in Confucianism through the term *chung-yung.* The word is often translated as the middle way, but it possesses a strong connotation of "timeliness," as in being neither too early nor too late, in a Confucian setting. Two indications of this, one in terms of human rights and the other in terms of human dignity, seem worth sharing. An op-ed piece appeared in the *New York Times* on February 5, 2002 under the title "Is the Human Rights Era Ending?" by Michael Ignatieff. It proposed that the time had come to challenge the regnant mood in the wake of the events of September 11, 2001, that "national security trumps human rights."[2] On the other hand, when the Śaṅkarācārya of Kāñcī, a leading pontiff of India, was asked, with tension building up in Ayodhyā for commencing work on the construction of the Rāma Temple on March 15, 2002: "What is the real meaning of ahiṁsā or non-violence in today's world?" he replied: "We need both pacifism and just wars for the good of the land,"[3] when such good presumably included maintaining human dignity, at least in the good land of India and perhaps the world.

One may now proceed by referring to one of the earliest episodes involving violence and dignity. It is provided by the Greek playwright Sophocles (496 BCE–406 BCE). "Human rights theorists refer to [his] Antigone, as the classic example from Greek literature. According to Sophocles, King Creon reproaches Antigone for having given her brother a burial, contrary to the law of the city (because her brother had fought against the Polis). She responded that she is obliged to follow a higher, unwritten law which supersedes positive (man-made) law."[4]

Hence one is tempted to ask: Do the dead have human rights—such as the right to a decent burial even at the hands of the enemy? Should a shared humanity not transcend enmity? It is here that the excerpted section from the *Rāmāyaṇa* becomes relevant. To recapitulate, as is well known, in the Hindu epic *Rāmāyaṇa*, the demon Rāvaṇa abducts the wife of Rāma and is ultimately killed by Rāma, as Rāma proceeds to rescue his wife Sītā from him. With Rāvaṇa lying dead, Rāma is asked what ought to be done with Rāvaṇa's dead body. Thereupon Rāma famously replies to the brother of the dead Rāvaṇa:

> Enmities end at death. Our purpose is served. Perform the proper rites. He is as much [a brother?] to me as he is to you.[5]

Violence comprises both human rights and human dignity. The matter seems fairly straightforward when stated in this way. But when it is put under an analytical lens, it gets more convoluted. It gets more convoluted in terms of human rights in view of the fact that sometimes it may be necessary to resort to violence in order to protect human rights—as in the face of terrorism. This is considered acceptable from a Hindu or even an Indic perspective, because this presents a case when violence recoils on violence, in the memorable phrase of the *Manusmṛti* (VIII.349–351), a well-known Hindu text usually assigned, in its present form, to the second century CE. Bühler translates the relevant verses as follows:

> 349. In their own defence, in a strife for the fees of officiating priests, and in order to protect women and brāhmaṇas; he who (under such circumstances) kills in the cause of right, commits no sin.

350. One may slay without hesitation an assassin who approaches (with murderous intent), whether (he be one's) teacher, a child or an aged man, or a brāhmaṇa deeply versed in the Vedas.
351. By killing an assassin the slayer incurs no guilt, whether (he does it) publicly or secretly; in that case fury recoils upon fury.[6]

These verses contain an important Sanskrit word, *ātatāyin*, literally one who has stretched the bow to the extreme, thereby graphically representing an oppressor. The word is also sometimes used in a technical sense to include the following six meanings: (1) an arsonist, (2) a murderer, (3) a terrorist, (4) a rapist, (5) a robber, and (6) a felon.[7]

We turn next to the question of human rights and human dignity *in* violence, namely in the conduct of violence or, briefly, in war. The *Manusmṛti* just alluded to also provides surprisingly relevant material on this point. The famous scholar of Indic civilization, Professor A. L. Basham, remarks on the provision relating to war found therein (VII.90–93) that the "chivalrous rules of warfare, probably based on a very old tradition, and codified in their present form among the martial peoples of western India in pre-Mauryan times, must have had some effect in mitigating the harshness of war for combatant and non-combatant alike."[8] He goes on to add: "it is doubtful if any other ancient civilization set such humane ideals of warfare."[9] Ideals, mind you—which means that they were perhaps not always observed in practice—but A. L. Basham was sufficiently impressed with them to write elsewhere in his classic study of Indic civilization: "No other ancient law giver proclaimed such noble ideals of fair play in battle as Manu did."[10]

Before we turn to the consideration of the ideals set for the combatants, let us pause for a moment to consider the fate of the noncombatants, who, according to the general code of war, were to be spared. Striking evidence that such was at least the case during some periods of ancient Indian history is provided by the extant fragments of the work of Megasthenes, the Seleucid ambassador at the court of the Mauryan emperor of India in the fourth century BCE. Megasthenes famously (though erroneously) observed that famine was unknown in India, meaning thereby perhaps that it was unknown in India as he knew it. This observation is remarkable in itself, but one of the explanations he provides for it is perhaps even more remarkable, for he goes on to say:

> But, further, there are usages observed by the Indians which contribute to prevent the occurrence of famine among them; for whereas among other nations it is usual, in the contests of war, to ravage the soil, and thus to reduce it to an uncultivated waste, among the Indians, on the contrary, by whom husbandmen are regarded as a class that is sacred and inviolable,

> the tillers of the soil, even when battle is raging in their neighbourhood, are undisturbed by any sense of danger, for the combatants on either side in waging the conflict make carnage of each other, but allow those engaged in husbandry to remain quite unmolested. Besides, they neither ravage an enemy's land with fire, nor cut down its tree.[11]

Hartmut Scharfe notes that "Alexander's historians observed with amazement how Indian peasants went about their work in the fields unharmed in full view of two fighting armies." He also notes that the *Mahābhārata* (XII.104.39) "recommends against the destruction of crops in war, at least under certain conditions, and tribal allies are instructed in the proper conduct of war [as follows]: don't destroy crops or fields."[12]

We turn next to the preservation of the dignity of the combatants themselves, or even of their human rights in some ways, speaking anachronistically of course.

> 90. When he fights with his foes in battle, let him not strike with weapons concealed (in wood), not with (such as are) barbed, poisoned, or the points of which are blazing with fire.
> 91. Let him not strike one who (in flight) has climbed on an eminence, nor a eunuch, nor one who joins the palms of his hands (in supplication), nor one who (flees) with flying hair, nor one who sits down, nor one who says "I am thine";
> 92. Nor one who sleeps, nor one who has lost his coat of mail, nor one who is naked, nor one who is disarmed, nor one who looks on without taking part in the fight, nor one who is fighting with another (foe);
> 93. Nor one whose weapons are broken, nor one afflicted (with sorrow), nor one who has been grievously wounded, nor one who is in fear, nor one who has turned to flight; (but in all these cases let him) remember the duty (of honorable warriors).[13]

Similar rules are also laid down in the epic *Mahābhārata* and elsewhere that, according to P. V. Kane, bear "comparison with the conventions of the Geneva and Hague Conferences."[14] It should be added, however, that the epic also provides instances of their violation.[15]

Battles end in either victory or defeat—no matter how they are fought. Sometimes the defeated king dies—but what if he survives? And what of his kingdom?

Hindu political theory provides a broad framework that helps answer such questions. It distinguishes between three types of conquests: "the first is conquest in which the defeated king is forced to render homage and tribute, after which he or a member of the family is reinstated as a vassal. The second is victory in which enormous booty is demanded and large portions of enemy territory annexed. The third involves the political annihilation of the conquered kingdom and its incorporation into that of the victor."[16]

The terms used to designate these three types of conquest are not without interest. The first, the least malevolent type, is called *dharma-vijaya* or righteous conquest; the second is called *lobha-vijaya* or larcenous or acquisitive conquest, in which booty is demanded; and the third, in which the ruler is ousted, is called *asura-vijaya* or demonic conquest, reminiscent of the ruthlessness of the Assyrians.

The idea of *dharma-vijaya* or righteous conquest is interesting. It was developed in certain circles to denote conquest only through righteousness, as by the Mauryan Buddhist emperor Aśoka; whereas in other circles it may have led to development of the perspective that came to view war as a ritual, on the analogy of the sacrifice of animals in Vedic ritual.[17]

Another term found in the Hindu tradition—analogous to that of *dharma-vijaya* or righteous conquest—is that of *dharma-yuddha* or righteous battle. An analysis of the word *dharma-yuddha* might help advance our discussion of violence and human dignity further. The word is a compound, in which the first word, *dharma*, means righteousness, along with a host of other meanings. The word *yuddha* means battle or war. As a compound expression it can be analyzed and made meaningful in more than one way. At the most obvious level, it could mean a righteous war, as well as a war fought righteously. That is to say, violence could be "dignified," either in terms of what it is being engaged in *for* or *how* it is being carried out. Thus "fighting may be noble or ignoble according to its purpose or object, so also it can be good or bad according to the manner in which it is carried out."[18] In other words, it could mean a just war or a war fought justly, and ideally both. Such a connotation imparts human dignity to an otherwise violent exercise, because justice rubs off on violence, as it were, in terms of both the means and end of violence, thereby dignifying both.

There is also a more specifically Hindu way of dignifying violence by placing it in the context of the so-called caste system. It is not often realized that one of the things performing one's inherited duty in life generated in Indian society was a sense of dignity. There was *also* a dignified way of discharging one's duty. In this sense, then, it was an honorable thing to be a warrior in itself. Then there was an honorable way of fighting. In this particular context, it meant not running away from battle or, as graphically stated in the tradition, "not showing one's back to the enemy." This fact of not running away from the field of battle is specifically mentioned in the *Bhagavadgītā* among the qualities of a *kṣatriya* and surfaces in the *Manusmṛti* (VII.89) also in the following verse:

> Those kings who, seeking to slay each other in battle, fight with the utmost exertion and do not *turn back*, go to heaven.[19]

This manner of fighting was also dignified soteriologically, to the extent that *what* one fought for became secondary to *how* one fought, namely, bravely. In the *Mahābhārata*, King Yudhiṣṭhira is one of the Pāṇḍava brothers. These Pāṇḍava brothers are the good guys, who win the war against the Kauravas, the evil cousins, who were the bad guys. After Yudhiṣṭhira died and was led into heaven, he was shocked to find the bad guys also in heavenm and it was explained to him that this was so because they performed their duty as *kṣatriyas*, or warriors, fittingly.

One feels a certain uneasiness perhaps with such an extension of the concept of dignity in relation to violence, and with good reason. For such an extension may explain a phenomenon that has puzzled cultural historians of India for a long time, namely, that, despite its commitment to ahiṁsā or non-violence, "positive condemnations of war are rare in Indian literature."[20] The same holds true of the death penalty. It is perhaps worth adding, just to emphasize this point, that this holds true even in the case of Jainism, whose commitment to ahiṁsā or non-violence is generally believed to exceed that of both Hinduism and Buddhism. The famous historian V. A. Smith found this point of sufficient consequence to include an explanation of it from a Jaina point of view in his history of India, which will not fail to interest us:

> A true Jaina will do nothing to hurt the feelings of another person, man, woman, or child; nor will he violate the principles of Jainism. Jaina ethics are meant for men of all positions—for kings, warriors, traders, artisans, agriculturists, and indeed for men and women in every walk of life . . . "Do your duty. Do it as humanely as you can." This, in brief, is the primary principle of Jainism. Non-killing cannot interfere with one's duties. The king, or the judge, has to hang a murderer. The murderer's act is the negation of a right of the murdered. The king's or the judge's, order is the negation of this negation, and is enjoined by Jainism as a duty. Similarly, the solder's killing on the battle-field.[21]

One suspects that one reason why in such cases violence may have lost its moral sting—its capacity to shock—may well be because it had been imbued with dignity in the ways previously discussed. Normally, we think of human rights and human dignity as morally synonymous concepts in human rights discourse. This graded discussion of violence in Hinduism, in the context of such discourse within it, generates the possibility that sometimes tension might arise between the two. A dignitarian approach to violence, for instance, might tend to justify it in contexts in which a rights-alone approach might consider it unjustified. A concept of the rights of the dead does not sound such a far-fetched concept from a dignitarian perspective.

Chapter 16

Human Rights, Human Dignity, and Alexander's Invasion of India

This chapter starts out, like the song of Wordsworth's Solitary Reaper, with "old unhappy far off things and battles long ago," as long ago as the time of Alexander the Great.

It might not seem exactly auspicious, and in fact even outright unpromising, to commence a discussion of human rights with an incident in the life of Alexander the Great. Perverse as it might appear, it seems the right course to follow. The West, of course, looks upon Alexander as a great conqueror, but many in the East look upon him as no more than another egregious violator of human rights. A widely read book on Indian history offers the following assessment of Alexander's invasion of India:

> The general Indian position with reference to the Macedonian invasion is well expressed by Matthew Arnold:
>
> "She let the legions thunder past, And plunged in thought again."
>
> The only permanent result of Alexander's campaign was that it opened up communication between Greece and India and paved the way for a more intimate intercourse between the two. And this was achieved at the cost of untold sufferings inflicted upon India—massacre, rapine and plunder on a scale till then without a precedent in her annals. In spite of the halo of romance that Greek writers have woven round the name of Alexander, the historian of India can regard him only as the precursor of these recognized scourges of mankind.[1]

Although these scourges detract form, rather than add, to human dignity, nevertheless it will now be proposed that Alexander's invasion might help us advance our discussion of human dignity, on the basis of a conversation he had with an Indian king the Greek sources call Porus, whom he defeated in a famous battle at the Hydaspes in 326 BCE. It is a battle studied even now at Westpoint and Sandhurst for the brilliant strategy employed therein by Alexander. We are, however, more concerned with what followed—after Porus had lost the battle and was captured:

> Alexander rode in front of the line with a few of the Companions to meet Porus; and stopping his horse, he admired his handsome figure and his stature, which reached somewhat above five cubits. He was also surprised that he did not seem to be cowed in spirit, but advanced to meet him as one brave man would meet another brave man, after having gallantly struggled in defence of his own kingdom against another king. Then indeed Alexander was the first to speak, bidding him say what treatment he would like to receive. The story goes that Porus replied: "Treat me, O Alexander, in a kingly way!" Alexander, being pleased at the expression, said: "For my own sake, O Porus, thou shalt be thus treated; but for thy own sake, do thou demand what is pleasing to thee!" But Porus said that everything was included in that. Alexander, being still more pleased at this remark, not only granted him the rule over his own Indians, but also added another country to that which he had before, of larger extent than the former. Thus he treated the brave man in a kingly way, and from that time found him faithful in all things.[2]

One needs to keep the crucial elements of the conversation in mind. To paraphrase: Alexander to Porus: How do you wish to be treated? Porus to Alexander: As a king treats a king. Alexander to Porus: Elaborate. Porus to Alexander: When I said as a king treats a king, everything was contained in that.

We have there, one dare say, an example of regal dignity. But we live in more democratic times, and perhaps that dignity, which was once the preserve of kings, may now be the possession not just of kings but of commoners as well.

Imagine now a situation in which a dissident is at the mercy of his torturer, and the torturer were to ask (in dark jest, perhaps), "Now, how do you wish to be treated?"—both knowing full well that the torturer had the power of life and death over the dissident. And the dissident were to say, "As a human being should treat another human being." And the torturer were to reply, "Elaborate your point." And the dissident were to say, "When I said treat me as a human being should treat another human being, everything was contained in that." Let us now regard this statement as an expression of human dignity and explore it from a religious perspective.

Several approaches could be brought to bear on the relationship between religion and human rights—a relationship that could be evaluated either positively or negatively or, more comprehensively and analytically, as including both possibilities. The remarks that follow take a *prima facie* positive view of this relationship. One may therefore begin by raising the question: In what way can religion be used as a positive resource in human rights discourse?

In framing this question, the word *religion* has been deliberately used in the singular. So the question to ask is not: In what way can religions be used as a positive resource in human rights discourse. Nor is the question identical to a similar question that one hears raised these days: In what ways can *world religions* be used as a positive resource for human rights? Both of these are rewarding questions. But these are not the questions being asked now. The question being asked now is: In what way can *religion*, in the singular, be used positively in thinking about human rights?

In attempting to answer this question, one might begin by trying to identify a feature of religion or religious experience in general. It is this. Somehow or other, religion links us and the world we live in with the transcendent—to something beyond us. Some have even argued that it is this transcendental dimension of religion that enables us to distinguish religion from ideology. Whether this is so, or what that transcendent is, or even *if* it is; these are questions of immense importance but that need not detain us here. One might wish to focus on this feature of transcendental linkage alone for the time being, for it seems to offer an important clue regarding how we might wish to think about human rights from a religious perspective.

Human rights discourse is at present largely juristic in its orientation. It primarily belongs to the realm of law, though not divorced from considerations of morality. This raises the following question in many minds. Given the way in which human rights discourse has come to dominate normative thinking in the public square, are human rights strong enough as a concept to bear the heavy weight we are placing on them? For if they are primarily a juristic concept, what the law gives, the law can take away—like the Lord. A society based *solely* on law is better, but perhaps only marginally better, than a society without it. In one, the letter of the law might kill, if lawlessness kills in the other. The matter could be put another way. Suppose the United Nations collapses tomorrow and the Universal Declaration of Human Rights becomes a dead letter. Could this mean that as human beings we would cease to possess human rights?

One senses a danger lurking here, the danger of aspiration becoming overly identified with an expression, a manifestation, of that aspiration, to the point that, if the manifestation is compromised, the aspiration itself may run the risk of being lost hold of—or at least lost sight of.

It is here that one might see some merit in introducing a transcendental dimension to the discourse. Such a transcendental dimension pervades religious discourse. At the most abstract level, the reality always transcends any manifestation of reality; at a theistic level, God transcends the universe; at a more concrete level, a religious tradition possesses a quality that exceeds or transcends its contents. One should not be misunderstood. One is not trying to smuggle religion in through the back door. What one is trying to do is to take into account the phenomenon described by Professor Charles Taylor as the suppression of ontology in modern pluralist and relativist culture. Let us, for instance, in pursuit of a firmer anchor for the concept of human rights, ask the question: What does a human being's humanity consist of?

Several answers are possible, answers on which even reasonable people might differ, to say nothing of unreasonable people.

The answers that have been offered to this question seem to either go too far or don't go far enough. It is tempting to anchor human rights, for instance, in religious or moral discourse. However, religions are characterized by ontological differences, and the search for moral universals is beset by various problems, so that to look for a religious or moral anchor compounds the problem. On the other hand, to place complete confidence in a merely legal conception of human rights alone, as complete and secure by itself, seems to leave too much in the hands of law. Even at a less elevated level, law cannot always be relied on even to secure justice in everyday life, without its ongoing and continuous scrutiny as a *means* of securing it.

We therefore need something less heavenly or lofty than religion or morality, but also less earth-bound or down-to-earth than just law. In such a situation the following suggestion is worth revisiting: that human rights be anchored in *human dignity*—not in God or morality or merely law—but in the concept of human dignity.

Human dignity as a concept can be related to human rights in at least three ways: (1) human dignity can be regarded as the product of the successful assertion of human rights; (2) or human dignity could be regarded as a partner-concept of human rights. One could then say, for instance, that participation in the political process enhances both human dignity *and* human rights, and (3) one could also regard human dignity as the *source* of human rights and consider human rights as flowing *from* human dignity. When one is operating with such evocative words as human dignity and human rights, which themselves possess multiple vectors of meaning, it should not come as a surprise that the relationship among them may be amenable to different patterns.

One could also link the three concepts: those of human dignity, human rights, and human duties in a specific way. The present model emphasizes the last of the three ways, in which the two concepts of human dignity and human rights may be related, namely, through human dignity as a source of human rights.

One may take one's cue from Aristotle's dictum that dignity does not consist in our receiving honors, but in our consciousness that we deserve them. If we replace the word *honors* by *rights* here, human dignity may be said to consist in our consciousness that we possess and deserve to possess, human rights, even when they are denied to us. This consciousness is coterminous with our consciousness of being a human being. Lest one feel that this involves splitting a particularly fine conceptual hair with little practical consequence, imagine a black rights activist in chains—she may have been deprived of her rights, but she is capable of experiencing and displaying human dignity. This is confirmed by the following observation:

> It is worth noting that much of the moral force of the civil-rights era of the early 1960s was achieved by blacks in the South—who, through the dignity and restraint of their personal behavior in the face of segregation's indignities, managed to transcend and shame—and ultimately defeat—a system designed to humiliate them.[3]

Once this interiority of human dignity is recognized as a psychic component of our make-up as a human being, which is independent of human rights but of which human rights constitute one particular recognition, the entire model may be presented as follows.

Human dignity inheres in all human beings *qua* human beings; human rights constitute one expression of it. Human dignity *is a quality* that is always present in, but is also more than and above, its various expressions.

Thus human dignity has to do with dignity that inheres in oneself as a human being and possesses a dimension of interiority as relating to one's self-perception. The *external* recognition of this dignity by another constitutes the basis of human rights. Respecting them devolves on the other party as *its* duty. In this way, human dignity, human rights, and human duty become intertwined in a web of relationships.

Take two human beings: A and B. Both possess human dignity within themselves in their awareness that they are human beings. B's recognition of this human dignity of A gives rise to A's human rights, which it is B's duty to respect. Similarly, it is A's duty to respect B's human rights, which flow from B's human dignity.

What have we accomplished through this exercise? The outcome may be demonstrated in terms of beneficiaries and obligors with the help of a classification developed by Professor Brian Lepard. Case 1: beneficiary—infant; obligor—mother. Let us now progressively enlarge the category. Case 2: beneficiary—children; obligor—parents. Case 3: beneficiaries—citizens; obligor—state. Case 4: beneficiaries—all human beings; obligors—all human beings, through rights-duty interface among them generated by the concept of human dignity.

It has been pointed out[4] that the same argument could be made in the parallel idiom of duties rather than rights. Take infants and mothers. The infant has a right to the mother's care, but once the infant grows up and the mother grows old, it becomes the grown-up infant's *duty* to take care of the mother. Again, children have rights vis-à-vis parents. But it is the *duty* of grown-up children to take care of their old parents. Again, citizens have rights against the state in normal times; in critical times it becomes the *duty* of the citizens—even through conscription—to protect the state. Finally, if all human beings have rights in relation to other human beings, the same holds true of duties.

Now that an outline of human rights discourse, as modeled on human dignity, has been presented, one is brought face to face with the inevitable question: How does this privileging of human dignity contribute to human rights discourse, if at all? An obvious advantage is the way in which the concept of human dignity allows one to intermesh rights and duties. Another less obvious, but equally clear-cut, advantage may lie in the fact that the concept of human dignity is similarly able to connect several generations of human rights discourse, those consisting of "'first generation' civil and political rights; 'second generation' social, cultural and economic rights, and 'third generation' environmental and developmental rights."[5] These are also sometimes referred to as distinct families of rights.[6] One could venture the opinion, from the perspective of human dignity, that, whereas the first generation rights—or more precisely "those norms therein which relate to physical and civil security (for example, no torture, slavery, [etc.])"[7] *recognize* human dignity; the rest *enhance* or enlarge it. Or one might say that the first generation rights treat *human dignity* as a *noun*, and those of the succeeding generations treat it as a *verb*. Three more points can now be developed beyond this point.

(1) The rise of human rights discourse in the West is closely associated with the rise of liberal secular thought. The secular location of this thought has not prevented scholars from wondering whether it might not be capable of a religious *extension*. As Ninian Smart and Shivesh Thakur have pointed out:

> An intriguing question arises as to whether differing cultures can arrive at a similar conclusion about rights by rather different routes—some via explicit philosophizing, as with Locke, Kant and others in the West; others by contemplating religious texts and duties (as in the *Mīmāṁsā* and *Gītā*); others again by exploiting ideas of ritual and performative behaviours towards others (e.g. *li* in China as a source of rights). It would be a happy outcome if so: since it would allow a confluence model of world society to establish itself—differing civilisations like so many rivers coming together, like the reverse of a delta.[8]

This creates room for suggesting that the idea of human dignity might enable one to build a bridge from the secular to the religious realm. For instance, Louis Henkin begins by claiming an exclusively secular provenance for human dignity when he writes:

> The human rights idea and ideology begin with an ur value or principle (derived perhaps from Immanuel Kant), the principle of human dignity. Human rights discourse has rooted itself in human dignity and finds its complete justification in that idea. The content of human rights is defined by what is required by human dignity—nothing less, perhaps nothing more.[9]

But he is careful to add parenthetically:

> (Some advocates of human rights may derive their commitment to human dignity from religious ideas or assumptions—for example, from the creation of persons by God in the image of God—but the human rights idea itself does not posit any religious basis for human dignity.)[10]

The point, however, was destined to break out of the parenthetical cage as well, for Henkin himself goes on to say later on in the same essay:

> Indeed some religions have begun to claim to be the source and the foundation, the progenitors, of the human rights idea, of the idea of human dignity that underlies it, of the commitment to justice that pervades it, of the bulk of its content. They have come to see human rights as natural rights rooted in natural law, natural law religiously inspired. The ancestors of the human rights idea, we are reminded, were religious Christians (Locke, Kant)—or at least deists (Jefferson). Religions have begun to welcome, and claim, human dignity as a religious principle implicit in teachings concerning the imago dei, the fatherhood of God, the responsibility for the neighbor. They have claimed as their own the concept of justice and its specifics: criminal justice, distributive justice, justice as fairness; some religions include economic and social rights as religious obligations. The

law of some religions has provided ingredients for particular human rights: for example, the right of privacy.[11]

(2) The concept of human dignity allows one to clarify the concept of human rights. The concept of universal human rights—famously enshrined in the Universal Declaration of Human Rights—suffers from a subtle ambiguity, which pertains to the relationship between the concepts of the *individual* and the *universal.* Often the two words are used interchangeably, but a significant, if subtle, difference also characterizes them. For instance, three statements can be made of an individual, any individual, such as you or I: (1) that an individual *is like no other,* that in some sense we all possess a unique identity; (2) that an individual is *like some others*; that is to say, we possess a group identity as citizens of a particular nation, or as belonging to a class, such as of academics, for instance; (3) that an individual is *like all others*; that is to say, we possess an identity coterminous with all human beings, as possessing a mind and body, etc.

It is only in this third sense that the individual and the universal overlap, which may explain the sense of unease some people might feel when women's rights are considered human rights, if in their minds the concept of human rights has been exclusively identified, or in their opinion should be exclusively identified, with the third sense.

Being human, however, involves all these three dimensions, and thus the juxtaposition of the words *human* and *universal* creates an ambiguity. Because being human involves all these three dimensions, the concept of human dignity also embraces all the three dimensions and enables us to understand the word *universal* in an extended sense—as embracing individual and *group differences* (because such differences characterize all human beings also), beyond their similarity in possessing in *common* what characterizes all human beings.

(3) The concept might also help us understand the relationship between religion and human rights better. For instance, Louis Henkin writes: "The human rights ideology, though it has not wholly outlawed capital punishment, clearly aims at its abolition because it derogates from human dignity—the dignity of the person executed, as well as the dignity of the members of the

> society that executes."[12] He then adds parenthetically: "It does not accept the argument that the human dignity of the victims of crime requires or justifies capital punishment."[13] Now, it is precisely in terms of the human dignity of the victims and of the members of the victim's family that an argument in support of capital punishment will be mounted by those who should wish to challenge human rights ideology on this point, as, for instance, the supporters of the provision of blood-compensation in Islamic law,[14] a practice that seems so recalcitrant to empathetic analysis at the first blush, until viewed in terms of the human dignity of the various parties involved, and especially of the victim's relatives.

The model of human dignity, human rights, and human duties, previously outlined, perhaps enables us to engage issues of human rights in a new way. It does not follow from this, however, that it solves all the problems associated with that discourse. To the extent that it enables us to come to grips with the issues more cogently, it may help toward achieving their resolution, but whether such a resolution is achieved or not depends on the case. Helping understand a problem better is not the same as solving it. There is all the difference in the world between the elucidation of a problem and its solution, but one may not disdain a better understanding of the problem, even if no solution might be yet forthcoming—especially if the probability of reaching one may be enhanced by such an improved understanding. In this spirit one might say that the concept of human dignity enables us to understand statements such as the following: "It can be affirmed that human rights are universal, but it is much more difficult to assert a universal standard of justice in upholding them."[15] This remark was prompted by what Bishop Tutu said during a visit to Edmonton, Canada, in his capacity as chairman of the Truth and Reconciliation Commission in South Africa.

> In Edmonton, Archbishop Tutu told a story of four men who had murdered young people in a small town. They appeared before his commission in the same town in a crowded hall before the very people whose relatives had been lost. They admitted their guilt. They expressed their remorse. They asked for forgiveness.
>
> It was a hot night. The hall had been filled with anger and passion. After some moments of silence, the crowd broke into applause and the guilty men wept. God was in the room that night, said Archbishop Tutu.[16]

One might like to raise the following question at this point: Dignity may well have been present in the room, but could it also be said that humanity was also present in the room? Were both divinity and humanity present in full measure, in some Christological way? Or could it be further asked: In exactly what way was human dignity present in the room? Had the human dignity of all been upheld, or had the human dignity of the victims been compromised, as some allege?

Appendix I

Universal Declaration of Human Rights

Adopted and Proclaimed by United Nations
General Assembly Resolution 217 (III)
On 10 December 1948

PREAMBLE

Whereas recognition of the inherent dignity and of the equal and inalienable rights of all members of the human family is the foundation of freedom, justice and peace in the world,

Whereas disregard and contempt for human rights have resulted in barbarous acts which have outraged the conscience of mankind, and the advent of a world in which human begins shall enjoy freedom of speech and belief and freedom from fear and want has been proclaimed as the highest aspiration of the common people,

Whereas it is essential, if man is not to be compelled to have recourse, as a last resort, to rebellion against tyranny and oppression, that human rights should be protected by the rule of law,

Whereas it is essential to promote the development of friendly relations between nations,

Whereas the peoples of the United Nations have in the Charter reaffirmed their faith in fundamental human rights, in the dignity and worth of the human person and in the equal rights of men and women and have determined to promote social progress and better standards of life in larger freedom,

Whereas Member States have pledged themselves to achieve, in co-operation with the United Nations, the promotion of universal respect for and observance of human rights and fundamental freedoms,

Whereas a common understanding of these rights and freedoms is of the greatest importance for the full realization of this pledge,

Now, therefore,
The General Assembly
Proclaims this Universal Declaration of Human Rights as a common standard of achievement for all peoples and all nations, to the end that every individual and every organ of society, keeping this Declaration constantly in mind, shall strive by teaching and education to promote respect for these rights and freedoms and by progressive measures, national and international, to secure their universal and effective recognition and observance, both among the peoples of Member States themselves and among the peoples of territories under their jurisdiction.

Article 1
All human beings are born free and equal in dignity and rights. They are endowed with reason and conscience and should act towards one another in a spirit of brotherhood.

Article 2
Everyone is entitled to all the rights and freedoms set forth in this Declaration, without distinction of any kind, such as race, colour, sex, language, religion, political or other opinion, national or social origin, property, birth or other status.

Furthermore, no distinction shall be made on the basis of the political, jurisdictional or international status of the country or territory to which a person belongs, whether it be independent, trust, non-self-governing or under any other limitation of sovereignty.

Article 3
Everyone has the right to life, liberty and security of person.

Article 4
No one shall be held in slavery or servitude; slavery and the slave trade shall be prohibited in all their forms.

Article 5
No one shall be subjected to torture or to cruel, inhuman or degrading treatment or punishment.

Article 6
Everyone has the right to recognition everywhere as a person before the law.

Article 7
All are equal before the law and are entitled without any discrimination to equal protection of the law. All are entitled to equal protection against any discrimination in violation of this Declaration and against any incitement to such discrimination.

Article 8
Everyone has the right to an effective remedy by the competent national tribunals for acts violating the fundamental rights granted him by the constitution or by law.

Article 9
No one shall be subjected to arbitrary arrest, detention or exile.

Article 10
Everyone is entitled in full equality to a fair and public hearing by an independent and impartial tribunal, in the determination of his rights and obligations and of any criminal charge against him.

Article 11
(1) Everyone charged with a penal offence has the right to be presumed innocent until proved guilty according to law in a public trial at which he has had all the guarantees necessary for his defence.
(2) No one shall be held guilty of any penal offence on account of any act or omission which did not constitute a penal offence, under national or international law, at the time when it was committed. Nor shall a heavier penalty be imposed than the one that was applicable at the time the penal offence was committed.

Article 12
No one shall be subjected to arbitrary interference with his privacy, family, home or correspondence, nor to attacks upon his honour and reputation. Everyone has the right to the protection of the law against such interference or attacks.

Article 13

(1) Everyone has the right to freedom of movement and residence within the borders of each state.
(2) Everyone has the right to leave any country, including his own, and to return to his country.

Article 14

(1) Everyone has the right to seek and to enjoy in other countries asylum from persecution.
(2) This right may not be invoked in the case of prosecutions genuinely arising from non-political crimes or from acts contrary to the purposes and principles of the United Nations.

Article 15

(1) Everyone has the right to a nationality.
(2) No one shall be arbitrarily deprived of his nationality nor denied the right to change his nationality.

Article 16

(1) Men and women of full age, without any limitation due to race, nationality or religion, have the right to marry and to found a family. They are entitled to equal rights as to marriage, during marriage and at its dissolution.
(2) Marriage shall be entered into only with the free and full consent of the intending spouses.
(3) The family is the natural and fundamental group unit of society and is entitled to protection by society and the State.

Article 17

(1) Everyone has the right to own property alone as well as in association with others.
(2) No one shall be arbitrarily deprived of his property.

Article 18

Everyone has the right to freedom of thought, conscience and religion; this right includes freedom to change his religion or belief, and freedom, either alone or in community with others and in public or private, to manifest his religion or belief in teaching, practice, worship and observance.

Article 19

Everyone has the right to freedom of opinion and expression; this right includes freedom to hold opinions without interference and to seek, receive and impart information and ideas through any media and regardless of frontiers.

Article 20

(1) Everyone has the right to freedom of peaceful assembly and association.
(2) No one may be compelled to belong to an association.

Article 21

(1) Everyone has the right to take part in the government of his country, directly or through freely chosen representatives.
(2) Everyone has the right of equal access to public service in his country.
(3) The will of the people shall be the basis of the authority of government; this will shall be expressed in periodic and genuine elections which shall be by universal and equal suffrage and shall be held by secret vote or by equivalent free voting procedures.

Article 22

Everyone, as a member of society, has the right to social security and is entitled to realization, through national effort and international co-operation and in accordance with the organization and resources of each State, of the economic, social and cultural rights indispensable for his dignity and the free development of his personality.

Article 23

(1) Everyone has the right to work, to free choice of employment, to just and favourable conditions of work and to protection against unemployment.
(2) Everyone, without any discrimination, has the right to equal pay for equal work.
(3) Everyone who works has the right to just and favourable remuneration ensuring for himself and his family an existence worthy of human dignity, and supplemented, if necessary, by other means of social protection.
(4) Everyone has the right to form and to join trade unions for the protection of his interests.

Article 24

Everyone has the right to rest and leisure, including reasonable limitation of working hours and periodic holidays with pay.

Article 25

(1) Everyone has the right to a standard of living adequate for the health and well-being of himself and of his family, including food, clothing, housing and medical care and necessary social services, and the right to security in the event of unemployment, sickness, disability, widowhood, old age or other lack of livelihood in circumstances beyond his control.

(2) Motherhood and childhood are entitled to special care and assistance. All children, whether born in or out of wedlock, shall enjoy the same social protection.

Article 26

(1) Everyone has the right to education. Education shall be free, at least in the elementary and fundamental stages. Elementary education shall be compulsory. Technical and professional education shall be made generally available and higher education shall be equally accessible to all on the basis of merit.

(2) Education shall be directed to the full development of the human personality and to the strengthening of respect for human rights and fundamental freedoms. It shall promote understanding, tolerance and friendship among all nations, racial or religious groups, and shall further the activities of the United Nations for the maintenance of peace.

(3) Parents have a prior right to choose the kind of education that shall be given to their children.

Article 27

(1) Everyone has the right freely to participate in the cultural life of the community, to enjoy the arts and to share in scientific advancement and its benefits.

(2) Everyone has the right to the protection of the moral and material interests resulting from any scientific, literary or artistic production of which he is the author.

Article 28

Everyone is entitled to a social and international order in which the rights and freedoms set forth in this Declaration can be fully realized.

Article 29

(1) Everyone has duties to the community in which alone the free and full development of his personality is possible.

(2) In the exercise of his rights and freedoms, everyone shall be subject only to such limitations as are determined by law solely for the purpose of securing due recognition and respect for the rights and freedoms of others and of meeting the just requirements of morality, public order and the general welfare in a democratic society.

(3) These rights and freedoms may in no case be exercised contrary to the purposes and principles of the United Nations.

Article 30

Nothing in this Declaration may be interpreted as implying for any State, group or person any right to engage in any activity or to perform any act aimed at the destruction of any of the rights and freedoms set forth herein.

Appendix II

Hinduism and Human Rights: A Critical Excursus

Current discourse on Hinduism and human rights is often reluctant to concede the possibility demonstrated in this book, that Hindu narratives on human rights could exist. The relationship between the two is presumed to be so antithetical that the effort undertaken here is bound to attract criticism along expected lines. I shall therefore, in this excursus, anticipate three such criticisms and try to meet them.

(1) **It is tendentious to seek to locate modern institutions or categories of thought in pre-modern history, as for instance, in the literature of classical Hinduism.**

The following points may be worth noting in this regard.

(1) Modernity is not merely a historical development, it has also evolved into an "ideology." And as an ideology, like all ideologies, it also tends to exaggerate its distinguishing features. One concept deeply embedded in modern self-perception is that of science. As a result, modern scholarship tends to play up the pre-scientific nature of medieval times and to contrast it with modern times, to the disadvantage of medieval times. It is widely held, for instance, that the medieval intellectual world believed in the existence of a flat earth. It has, however, now been demonstrated that this is largely a modern construct about medieval times.[1] This creates room for suggesting that a similar process may be at work in humanities as well, and not just in the sciences.

(2) There are instances where ideas found in ancient India have a very modern flavor to them. Bultmann proposed a way of

studying Christian religious scriptures in the last century, which is often referred to as "demythologizing." K. Satchidananda Murty noted years ago that this position is anticipated by Kumārila and Śaṅkara. He says quite clearly: "It is a great tribute to the ancient Hindu thinkers that principles of scriptural exegesis somewhat similar to theirs are now being advocated by some of the foremost Christian theologians; to wit, the powerful movement of *entmythologisierung* inaugurated by Prof. Bultmann."[2]

Are we to disregard this evidence on the assumption that *ancient* thinkers could not have adopted such a *modern* position? It is not being suggested that sometimes parallels may not have been forced, and it is our task as scholars to detect them. But it is also our duty as scholars to look at the evidence, rather than discard that evidence on the basis of a presumption.

(3) A special point needs to be kept in mind when dealing with a tradition such as Hinduism, whose plural character has been widely acknowledged. The fact that a tradition allows many points of view to coexist means that the probability of some such point of view coinciding with a modern point of view will be greater, in comparison to another tradition that allows for a more limited set of possible views.

An illustration might help advance the point. The world is said to rest on a tortoise, according to certain Puranic theories. And if it is asked "On what does the turtle rest"? one might be told that it is turtles all the way. The same Hindu tradition, however, also provides room for Vedantic doctrines of creation. Thus the Hindu religious tradition provides scope for many diverse doctrines. The earth is seen as resting on a turtle at one end of the spectrum, at the other end, "the extraordinary scope of the Hindu imagination is illustrated by the fact that the great Indian commentator Rāmānuja, who lived in the eleventh century C.E., placed the date of Vivasvat's birth at twenty-eight mahāyugas (about 120 billion years ago) before his time, a figure which is perhaps closer to modern scientific theories about the birth of the sun than the chronologically vague account in Genesis would place it."[3]

Is the scholar who points the latter fact abetting Hindu chauvinism, and the one who refers to the former account primitivizing Hinduism? It is possible to accuse them of being tendentious, but it is also possible to maintain that both are presenting verifiable facts, which it would be dangerous to ignore on the mere assumption of tendentiousness. Perhaps attention should be directed toward the comprehensive nature of the tradition one is dealing with, rather to their alleged tendentiousness.

Even popular textbooks on philosophy note that, although, "in the history of Western philosophy we usually find the different schools coming into existence successively," "in India, on the other hand, we find that the different schools, though not originating simultaneously, flourish together during many centuries, and pursue parallel courses of growth."[4] This observation takes the argument beyond its previous limits. Not only may a plural tradition contain many elements, it is also often able to keep these many elements open as live rather than archival options.

Such being the nature of the tradition, it should not come as a surprise that it would contain *elements that might be capable of being aligned with both the most regressive, as well as the most progressive features of modernity.*

The point one wishes to make is that the question whether modern institutions or categories are prefigured in pre-modern times cannot be settled on the a priori assumption that these could not have been *prefigured* in pre-modern times, because we consider them modern. Is Professor A. L. Basham being tendentious when he writes as follows:

> The testimony of Megathenes, corroborated by the *Arthaśāstra*, shows that in Mauryan times prices were regulated by market officials. The latter text suggests that, as a further effort at maintaining a just price, government officers should buy on the open market when any staple commodity was cheap and plentiful, and release stocks from government stores when it was in short supply, thus bringing down the price and making a profit for the king in the bargain. We have no evidence that this idea was ever put into effect, but it is striking that ancient Indian political theorists anticipated by over 2,000 years the plans put forward by the Food and Agriculture Organization of the United Nations for maintaining a stable level of prices of staple commodities on a world-wide scale.[5]

One should of course not project onto ancient institutions ideas that are distinctly modern, but we should also not commit the opposite error—of denying comparable elements when they are present. One certainly needs to be judicious, even cautious, in the spirit found in the following comments by A. L. Basham, wherein he examines the appropriateness of designating certain political institutions in India as "republics":

> The term "republic" is often used for these bodies, and though it has been criticized by some authorities, it is quite legitimate if it is remembered that the *gaṇas,* or tribes, were not governed like the Republic of India by an assembly elected by universal suffrage. The Roman Republic was not a democracy, but it was a republic nevertheless, and the evidence shows that

in some of these ancient Indian republican communities a large number of persons had some say in the government.[6]

Consider the case of slaves for instance. If it turns out that "in no other ancient lawbook are their rights so well protected as in the *Arthaśāstra*,"[7] should we overlook this evidence because we have already hypothesized that the ancient world was too ridden with slavery for this to happen? It would be tendentious to do so.

(2) There is reason to believe that the classical Hindu tradition, deeply differentiated and context-ridden in its social and moral outlook, could not have evolved a universally applicable paradigm of the "human," inherent in human rights discourse.

This is the crux of the matter. In order to do it justice, I shall first discuss whether classical Hindu tradition did evolve a universal paradigm, although, even in our times, it is a *contested point whether "human rights" constitute a universal paradigm.*[8] I, however, do not wish to press the point regarding the putative universality of human rights further, for fear that it would become a red herring, but confine myself to the consideration that universal paradigms are not likely to arise from within the kind of differentiated outlook that characterizes the classical Hindu tradition.

Such a universal perspective however *did* arise in classical Hindu tradition, and it is referred to therein as *sāmānya dharma*, *sādhāraṇa dharma*, or *sāmāsika dharma*. It is also sometimes referred to as *sanātana dharma*. This point needs to be grasped carefully because available writings on classical Hinduism often miss this point. A. L. Basham acknowledges the existence of this universal dimension *twice* in his celebrated *magnus opus*, but without mentioning the name for it:

> There is indeed a common Dharma, a general norm of conduct which all must follow equally.[9]
>
> Certain broad principles applied to all sections of the community, but beyond these no detailed code of morality was universally binding.[10]

At a third place, where he could (and should?) have acknowledged it, he does not seem to:

> *Dharma* . . . in legal literature . . . may perhaps be defined as the divinely ordained norm of good conduct, varying according to class and caste.[11]

The first edition of Professor A. L. Basham's book appeared in 1954 and was subsequently revised in 1963 and 1967. But even as late as 1988 this category fails to register in many a work. Wilhelm Halbfass, in his influential work *India and Europe: An Essay in Understanding*[12] refers to the concept of *sādhāraṇa dharma* at three places[13] but insists that it is either "peripheral,"[14] or that, for it, "what is 'common' to mankind at large is of no real concern."[15]

Thus Basham refers to the concept but not the word; Halbfass refers to the word but not the concept. Whether this treatment is justified is for the reader to judge on the basis of the following evidence.

One may begin by citing Professor P. V. Kane on this point, whose monumental multivolume *History of Dharmaśāstra* is now the standard work in the field. In the penultimate chapter to the book entitled: "Fundamental and Leading Characteristics and Conceptions of Hindu Culture and Civilization," he writes:

> Apart from the specific qualities required to be possessed by the members of each of the four varṇas, all *Dharmaśāstra* works attach the highest importance to certain moral qualities and enjoin them on all men. Manu X.63, Yāj. I.22, Gaut. Dh. S. VIII.23–25, Matsya 52.8–10 (quoted above on p. 1023 n. 1652) prescribe for all Varṇas a brief code of morals, such as ahiṃsā, truthfulness, non-stealing (i.e. no wrongful taking of another's property), purity and restraint of the senses. The Mitākṣarā on Yāj. I.22 explains that the word "sarveṣām" therein states that these moral qualities if practiced are the means of Dharma for all men from brāhmaṇas to cāṇḍālas. Vide H. of Dh. Vol. II. pp. 10–11 for different enumerations of dharmas common to all men.[16]

That the *Dharmaśāstra* texts attach great importance to *sādhāraṇa* or *sāmānya* dharma, or duties incumbent on all, is obvious from even such a "deeply differentiated and context-ridden" text as the *Manusmṛti*. After enumerating the duties of the various *varṇas*, at one point the *Manusmṛti* states (X.63):

> Abstention from injuring, truthfulness, refraining from anger, purification, and mastering the organs—this, Manu has declared, is the gist of the Law for the four classes.[17]

Similarly, after enumerating the duties of the various *āśramas*, the *Manusmṛti* states (VI.91–93):

> Resolve, forbearance, self-control, refraining from theft, performing purifications, mastering the organs, understanding, learning, truthfulness, and suppressing anger: these are the ten points of the Law.[18]

The deeply differentiated character of Hindu ethics is said to be encapsulated in the term *varṇāśrama dharma*. It therefore cannot be an insignificant matter that, in the course of his discourse on *both* of them, *varṇa* as well as *āśrama*, the *Manusmṛti* does not fail to draw attention to *sādhāraṇa dharma*.

The *Brahmapurāṇa* (114.18) explicitly states that these *dharmas* are common to all *varṇas* and *āśramas* (*sāmānyā varṇānāṁ kathitā guṇāḥ. āśramāṇāṁ ca sarveṣāmete sāmānya-lakṣaṇāḥ*).[19] The importance of the citation from the *Brahmapurāṇa* is twofold: (1) it indicates that the enumeration of these common *dharmas* is not confined to the *smṛtis*, but also occurs in the Purāṇas; (2) that *sādhāraṇa* dharmas are not only mentioned in the context of *varṇa* and *āśrama* duties when they are mentioned separately, but that they are also mentioned when *varṇāśrama* duties are enjoined jointly.

It is also worth noting that the enumeration of these *sādhāraṇa dharmas* is not limited to "religious" texts. They figure in a secular text, such as the *Arthaśāstra* (I.3.13)[20] on the one hand, and in texts of yoga on the other, such as Patañjali's *Yogasūtra* (II.30–31).[21]

How the inclusion or exclusion of this category of *sādhāraṇa dharma* affects the discussion of Hindu ethics may be illustrated with the help of two examples.

For the first, I turn to the discussion of Hindu ethics found in Donald Eugene Smith's standard work: *India as a Secular State* (1963). Chapter 11 of this book is entitled "Caste and the Secular State," and the discussion of the concept of *dharma* within it is totally innocent of the dimension of *sāmānya dharma* or duties common to all.[22] As a result, the otherwise informed and sensitive discussion takes no cognizance of the universal component of Hindu ethics. The heavy reliance of Donald Eugene Smith on Max Weber, who similarly overlooks this dimension of Hinduism,[23] is a good example of how the neglect perpetrated by one scholar is unwittingly perpetuated by another. It is this neglect that has perhaps contributed to the view that Hindu dharma does not take common humanity into account and is restricted to the performance of caste duties.

Julius Lipner in his *Hindus: Their Religious Beliefs and Practices* (1994) does take the category of *sādhāraṇa* or *sāmānya dharma* into account, with the result that his treatment diverges from that of those scholars who don't. He writes:

> Further, also exerting a strong influence on how one was to behave morally was what may be called *sādhāraṇa dharma*, namely, general morality (as opposed to *svadharma*). The Law Codes also imply or speak of a general

> morality. We read in Manu: "Non-injury (*āhiṃsā*), truth (*satya*), not stealing (*asteya*), purity (*śáuca*), control of the senses (*indriyanigraha*)—Manu has declared this to summarise *dharma* for the four castes" (10.63). The *Vāsiṣṭha* Law Code says: "Avoiding backbiting, envy, pride, egoism, unbelief, guile, boasting, insulting others, hypocrisy, greed, infatuation, anger and discontent is approved *dharma* for all the stages of life." This would have been directed first at the "twice-born," but it was to apply to all within the pale of "Hindu" *dharma*, women, low castes and untouchables as well. This application would not be straightforward, but required careful attention to circumstances. We may illustrate this by reference to the virtue of non-injury (*ahiṃsā*).[24]

Once this category of *sāmānya dharma* is taken into account, the nature of the discussion is fundamentally affected. Whereas earlier on, when the discussion was conducted without factoring *sādhāraṇa dharma* into the analysis, Hindu ethical issues were presented as representing a study in contrast between the particularity of Hindu ethics and the universality of Western ethics. Once this category is taken cognizance of, the issue is transformed into one of the manner in which Hindu ethics negotiates the universal and the particular dimensions. The difference may be illustrated with the actual case of Suttee (or Satī). According to the earlier view Suttee (or Satī) is just a *strīdharma*, like so many particular *dharmas* of Hinduism, such as *varṇāśrama-dharma* or *rājadharma*. With the help of a lens that recognizes the presence of *sādhāraṇa dharma* within Hinduism, the discussion proceeds as follows:

> Let us also consider the recommendation to practice suttee, a suicidal form of self-injury. According to some authorities this was generally a good thing for wives just widowed, but exceptions were made. Thus the *Mitākṣarā*, the most authoritative and well-known commentary (eleventh to twelfth century) on the *Yājñavalkyasmṛti* (see Chapter 4), recommends, but does not enforce, suttee on all wives, including the Caṇḍāla (one of the most despised castes; "*ā caṇḍālam*," says the text) *provided that* they are not pregnant or have young children to look after (1.86). Thus suttee overrides the directive to practice *ahiṃsā*, but the value accorded to new and vulnerable life outweighs the directive to practice suttee. Note that the text includes the Caṇḍāla within the scope of this dharmic injunction; the Caṇḍāla wife is enjoined both to commit suttee and to desist, depending on circumstances. So the conflict between *sādhāraṇa dharma* and *svadharma*, and the need to resolve it, apply to her no less than to the twice-born.[25]

This has a direct bearing on the discussion in the preceding pages of the book. One may be skeptical of classical Hinduism having anything to offer to human rights discourse if one believed that Hindu ethics is only particularistic. But if we do not overlook the category of *sādhāraṇa dharma*, a universal dimension within classical Hindu ethic will have to be accepted, and with it the possibility that classical Hindu ethics could possibly resonate with and contribute to human rights discourse.

(3) Can one really believe that some critical and civil questions, which first emerged in modern Europe and then influenced thinking in the third world, were actually already anticipated in classical Hinduism?

It is not, however, being proposed that the issues pertaining to human rights discourse were already fully anticipated as such in classical Hinduism. It is, rather, being proposed that these issues are not such as were entirely unanticipated, in some measure, in the literature associated with classical Hinduism. That this may even be true of Hindu folklore is suggested by the following account:

> [This] is the story of Siddharaj Jaisinh (12th century), the king of Gujarat, widely known for his fairness and justice. Jaisinh's mother, Minaldevi, who was from Karnataka, was on her way to Somanath. Passing through the dry area in central Gujarat she saw that many pilgrims and travelers were having great difficulty in finding water. She asked Jaisinh to build a lake in that area. Siddharaj is known for having built lakes and step-wells, including the famous Sahasralinga lake in Patan. He had his architects made a plan for a lake in present day Dholka. The plan was for a circular lake. An old widow's hut stood at the site where the lake was to be dug. She was requested to sell her land and hut to the king; but she refused. When she did not change her mind even after many attempts to convince her, the king ordered that the lake be built circumventing her hut. The lake was built with an uneven circumference. The lake is still in existence. At the spot where the old woman's hut stood, stands a plaque telling the story.[26]

Should this story not constitute evidence of human rights thinking in ancient India, after what we have read in Chapter 4 of this book?

Notes

INTRODUCTION

1. See Michael Ignatieff, *The Rights Revolution* (Toronto: Canadian Broadcasting Corporation, 2000), Chapter I.
2. Ian Brownlie, ed., *Basic Documents on Human Rights* (third edition) (Oxford: Clarendon Press, 1992), pp. 21–27.
3. Mary Ann Glendon, *A World Made New: Eleanor Roosevelt and the Universal Declaration of Human Rights* (New York: Random House, 2001), p. 121.
4. Joseph Runzo, *Global Philosophy of Religion: A Short Introduction* (Oxford: Oneworld, 2001), pp. 180, 188.
5. A. L. Basham, *The Wonder That Was India* (New Delhi: Rupa & Co., 1999[1954]), pp. 113, 137, 340; Wilhelm Halbfass, *India and Europe: An Essay in Understanding* (Albany: State University of New York Press, 1981), pp. 333, 509 note 28; Axel Michaels, *Hinduism: Past and Present* (translated by Barbara Harshav (Princeton and Oxford: Princeton University Press, 2004), pp. 16; and others.
6. P. V. Kane, *History of Dharmaśàstra* Vol. V Part II (second edition) (Poona: Bhandarkar Oriental Research Institute, 1977), pp. 1637ff.
7. Joseph Runzo, op. cit., p. 173.
8. T. M. P. Mahadevan, *Outlines of Hinduism* (Bombay: Chetana Limited, 1971), p. 103.
9. Jonardon Ganeri, ed., *The Collected Essays of Bimal Krishna Matilal: Ethics and Epics* (Delhi: Oxford University Press, 2002), p. 109.
10. For the discussion in analytical form, please refer to my *Hinduism and Human Rights: A Conceptual Approach* (New Delhi: Oxford University Press, 2003).

CHAPTER 1

1. Alan Dershowitz, *Rights from Wrongs: A Secular Theory of the Origins of Rights* (New York: Basic Books, 2004), p. 90.
2. For the human rights implications of the exemption of Brahmins from the death penalty, see Arvind Sharma, *Hinduism and Human Rights: A Conceptual Approach* (New Delhi: Oxford University Press, 2003), p. 71.
3. Todd S. Purdum, "The Supreme Court's Biggest Question," *New York Times,* Sep. 18, 2005, Section 4, p. 1.
4. Purdum, "The Supreme Court's Biggest Question."
5. Purdum, "The Supreme Court's Biggest Question."
6. Ainslie T. Embree, ed., *Sources of Indian Tradition,* 2nd ed. (New York: Columbia University Press, 1988), p. 508.

CHAPTER 2

1. Isaiah Berlin, *Four Essays on Liberty* (New York: Oxford University Press, 1969), p. 129, emphasis added.
2. Cited in Robert Traer, *Faith in Human Rights: Support in Religious Traditions for a Global Struggle* (Washington, DC: Georgetown University Press, 1991), pp. 150–51.
3. Arvind Sharma, *Hinduism and Human Rights: A Conceptual Approach* (New Delhi: Oxford University Press, 2003), pp. 61–63.
4. John B. Carman, "Duties and Rights in Hindu Society," in Leroy S. Rouner, ed., *Human Rights and the World's Religions* (Notre Dame, IN: University of Notre Dame Press, 1988), p. 121.
5. Rouner, "Duties and Rights in Hindu Society," p. 1.
6. Cited by Traer, *Faith in Human Rights,* pp. 131–32.
7. J. A. B. van Buitenen, trans., *The Mahàbhàrata* (Chicago and London: The University of Chicago Press, 1975), vol. 2, p. 137.
8. On the significance of the warrior's honor, even in our times, see Michael Ignatieff, *The Warrior's Honour* (New York: Henry Holt & Company, 1997), passim.
9. R. S. Sharma, *Aspects of Political Ideas and Institutions in Ancient India* (Delhi: Motilal Banarsidass, 1968), p. 97, emphasis added.
10. Sharma, *Aspects of Political Ideas,* p. 98, emphasis added.
11. Jonarden Ganeri, ed., *The Collected Essays of Bimal Krishna Matilal: Ethics and Epics* (Delhi: Oxford University Press, 2002) p. 115.

CHAPTER 3

1. T. Patrick Burke, *No Harm: Ethical Principles for a Free Market* (New York: Paragon House, 1994), p. 15.
2. Burke, *No Harm,* p. 16.
3. Burke, *No Harm.,* p. 17.

4. T. M. P. Mahadevan, *Outlines of Hinduism* (Bombay: Chetana Limited, 1971), p. 91.
5. Mahadevan, *Outlines of Hinduism.*
6. A. C. Bhaktivedanta Swami Prabhupàda, *Śrīmad Bhàgavatam* (New York: The Bhaktivedanta Book Trust, 1976) Seventh Canto, Part I, p. 165.
7. The phrase can also be construed differently.

CHAPTER 4

1. Michael Ignatieff, *The Rights Revolution* (Toronto: Canadian Broadcasting Corporation, 2000), p. 4.
2. Alan Dershowitz, *Rights from Wrongs: A Secular Theory of the Origins of Rights* (New York: Basic Books, 2004), p. 53.
3. Dershowitz, *Rights from Wrongs.*
4. Ignatieff *The Rights Revolution,* pp. 24–25.
5. R. C. Majumdar, ed., *The Vedic Age* (London: George Allen & Unwin, 1952), p. 49.
6. R. C. Majumdar, *Ancient India* (Delhi: Motilal Banarsidass, 1964), p. 261.
7. M. A. Stein, *Kalhaṇa's Rājataraṅgiṇī: A Chronicle of the Kings of Kasmār* (Delhi: Banarsidass, 1984 [1900]), vol. I, pp. 74–75.
8. Stein, *Kalhaṇa's Rājataraṅgiṇī,* p. 323.
9. Stein, *Kalhaṇa's Rājataraṅgiṇī,* pp. 237–39.

CHAPTER 5

1. Bhikhu Parekh, "The Modern Conception of Right and Its Marxist Critique", in Upendra Baxi, ed., *The Right to Be Human* (New Delhi: Lancer International, 1987), p. 8.
2. Parekh, "The Modern Conception of Right, p. 8.
3. Mary Ann Glendon, *A World Made New: Eleanor Roosevelt and the Universal Declaration of Human Rights* (New York: Random House, 2000), p. xvii.
4. Glendon, *A World Made New.*
5. Glendon, *A World Made New.*
6. Glendon, *A World Made New.*
7. Ian Brownlie, ed., *Basic Documents on Human Rights,* Third Edition (Oxford: Clarendon Press, 1994), p.25.
8. Ian Brownlie, ed., *Basic Documents on Human Rights,* p.26.
9. Patrick Olivelle, *The Law Code of Manu* (New York: Oxford University Press, 2004) p. 19.
10. Olivelle, *The Law Code of Manu,* p. 191.
11. See J. Duncan M. Derrett, *Religion, Law and State in India* (New York: The Free Press, 1968), p. 96.
12. Olivelle, *The Law Code of Manu,* p. 191.

13. P. V. Kane, *History of Dharmaśàstra,* vol. II, Part I, pp. 120–21.
14. Olivelle, *The Law Code of Manu,* p. 187.
15. Ollivelle, *The Law Code of Manu,* p. 188.

CHAPTER 6

1. Stanley I. Benn, "Equality Moral and Social", in Paul Edwards, Editor in Chief, *The Encyclopedia of Philosophy* (New York: The Macmillan Company and Free Press, 1967), vol. 7, p. 198.
2. See Paul Gordon Lauren, *The Evolution of International Human Rights: Visions Seen* (Philadelphia: University of Pennsylvania Press, 1998), Chapter 2.
3. Arvind Sharma, *Hinduism and Human Rights: A Conceptual Approach* (New Delhi: Oxford University Press, 2003), p. 39. Also see Asha Bajpai, *Child Rights in India: Law, Policy, and Practice* (New Delhi and New York: Oxford University Press, 2003).
4. See Arti Dhand, "The Subversive Nature of Virtue in the *Mahàbhàrata*: A Tale About Women, Smelly Ascetics, and God," *Journal of the American Academy of Religion* 71:1:33–58 (March 2004).
5. According to the *Arthaśāstra* of Kauṭilya, Māṇḍavya, though really not a thief, declared that he was so through fear of torture. The actual Sanskrit expression used runs as follows: *karma-kleśa-bhayàt* or out of fear of the torment of torture. The word karma here means torture; see P. V. Kane, *History of Dharmaśàstra* (Poona: Bhandarkar Oriental Research Institute, 1973), vol. III (2nd ed.), p. 255, note 332. He goes on to note: "The story of Māṇḍavya, who though not a thief was held to be a thief, because he, owing to his vow of silence, did not reply when questioned and near whom was found the booty stolen and who was impaled, is found in âdi. 63.92–93 (cr. ed. chap. 57), âdi 107–108 (cr. ed. chap. 101), Anuśàsana 18.46–50 and in Nàr, (I.42) and Bç. quoted by Aparàrka (p. 599). Kauṭ. IV.8 appears to have had a different version of the story before him. The Màrkaṇḍeyapuràṇa (chap. 16) has the story of Aṇāmàtóavya. The story of Māṇḍavya was a leading case, it appears, in criminal law."
6. M. A. Stein, trans., *Kalhaṇa's Rājataraṅgiṇī: A Chronicle of the Kings of Kaśmīr* (Delhi: Motilal Banarsidass, 1989 [1903]), vol. I, pp. 77–78.
7. John B. Carman, "Duties and Rights in Hindu Society", in Leroy S. Rouner, ed., *Human Rights and the World's Religions* (Notre Dame, Indiana: University of Notre Dame Press, 1988), pp. 116–17.
8. Carman, "Duties and Rights, p. 117.
9. Carman, "Duties and Rights, p. 117–18.
10. See P. V. Kane and C. N. Joshi, *Uttararàmacarita of Bhavabhūti* (Delhi: Motilal Banarsidass, 1962), p. 39.
11. Kane and Joshi, *Uttararàmacarita,* p. 39.

CHAPTER 7

1. Qureshi, cited in Werner F. Menski, *Hindu Law: Beyond Tradition and Modernity* (New Delhi: Oxford University Press, 2003), p. 282.
2. Menski, *Hindu Law.*
3. Menski, *Hindu Law.*
4. See John B. Carman, "Duties and Rights in Hindu Society", in Leroy S. Rouner, ed., *Human Rights and the World's Religions* (Notre Dame, Indiana: University of Notre Dame Press, 1988), p. 121.
5. The classical form Duṣyanta has been preferred over the epic form Duḥyanta for simplicity.
6. Stephanie W. Jamison translates these lines for emphasis as follows: "You yourself are your own relative. You yourself are your own means. You ought to make a *gift of yourself* by yourself according to law" (*Sacrificed Wife/Sacrificer's Wife: Women, Ritual, and Hospitality in Ancient India* [New York and Oxford: Oxford University Press, 1996], p. 214).
7. Is it so called because the *gandharvas* are said to be its witnesses? In any case the *gàndharva* form of marriage is said to be the best in general according to the *Kàmasūtra* (III.5.61). Also see *Baudhàyana Dharma Sūtra* I.11.13.7.

CHAPTER 8

1. "Sàvitrī tells Death she must follow her dead husband because such is the immemorial custom of the wife," so Peter Heehs, "The Centre of the Religious and Cultural Nationalism in the Work of Sri Aurobindo," in Antony Copley, ed., *Hinduism in Public and Private: Reform, Hindutva, Gender, Sampraday* (New Delhi: Oxford University Press, 2003), p. 70.
2. Glendon, *A World Made New,* p. 312.
3. Menski, *Hindu Law,* p. 330.
4. This, at least in theory, seems to have been a daughter's *right,* that she could choose a man for herself right after puberty if her parents failed to find one. Some versions of the *Pañcatantra* contain a story in which the wife urges the husband to obtain a husband for the daughter who has now reached puberty, because, if he won't do so, she will find one on her own because: "When a girl remains in her paternal home after menstruation, it is laid down that she should offer herself to a husband, choose her husband"; see M. R. Kale, *Pañcatantra of Viṣṇuśarman* (Delhi: Motilal Banarsidass, 1986), p. 475. The Sanskrit verse, reproduced as follows, attributes this position to Manu (M.R. Kale, *Pañcatantra,* p.227):

   ṛtumatyàm tu tiṣṭhantyàm svecchàdànam vidhāyate
   tasmàdudvàhayennagnàm manuḥ syàyambhuvo'bravīt.

5. Italics added.

CHAPTER 9

1. A. L. Basham, *The Wonder That Was India* (New Delhi: Rupa & Co., 1999) p. 430 (note).
2. A.L. Basham, *The Wonder That Was India,* pp. 429–30.

CHAPTER 10

1. Alan Dershowitz, *Rights from Wrongs: A Secular Theory of the Origin of Rights* (New York: Basic Books, 2004), p. 193.
2. A. L. Basham, "Hinduism", in R. C. Zaehner, ed., *The Concise Encyclopedia of Living Faiths* (Boston: Beacon Press, 1967), p. 225.
3. Dershowitz, *Rights from Wrongs,* pp. 197–99.
4. Dershowitz, *Rights from Wrongs,* p. 198.
5. The following remarks of Alan Dershowitz, in keeping with his "experiential approach" are worth bearing in mind here (Dershowitz, *Rights from Wrongs,* p. 199): "The strongest case for animal rights derives from the history and experiences of human beings. Societies that treat animal life with greater respect tend also to treat human life with greater respect. It is preferable to live in a society that seeks to limit the suffering of animals than in one that does not. This does not necessarily mean that a vegetarian society will always be better than a carnivorous one. Hitler, it is said, was a vegetarian, and the Nazi SS surely treated their dogs better than they treated the Jews and Gypsies. Nor is it an argument against necessary medical experimentation on animals, since history and experience have shown that societies that take an animal life to preserve human life can be good and caring places in which to live—at least for humans! It is merely a claim that the gratuitous infliction of pain on animals is bad for humans, and its toleration is bad for any human society. This is the soft case for a human-centered approach to animal rights. It requires that when human beings balance their perceived needs against the interests of animals, we must take into account their suffering and seek to minimize it (as we should take into account and try to minimize environmental damage when we create jobs and businesses)."
6. I am indebted to Dr. Shrinivas Tilak for alerting me to the rights dimension of this incident.
7. For Sanskrit text, see Subodhacandra Pant, *Abhijñànaśàkuntalam* (Delhi: Motilal Banarsidass, 1995), pp. 20–39.

CHAPTER 11

1. Ian Brownlie, ed., *Basic Documents on Human Rights,* Third Edition (Oxford: Clarendon Press, 1994), p. 26.
2. For Sanskrit text, see P. V. Kane and C. N. Joshi, *Uttararàmacarita of Bhavabhūti* (Delhi: Motilal Banarsidass, 1962), pp. 32–35, emphasis supplied.

3. A. S. Altekar, *The Position of Women in Hindu Civilization from Prehistoric Times to the Present Day* (Delhi: Motilal Banarsidass, 1995 [1959]), p. 10, diacritics revised.
4. Altekar, *The Position of Women,* also see P. V. Kane, *History of Dharmaśāstra* (Poona: Bhandarkar Oriental Research Institute, 1974), vol. II, Part I (2nd ed.), p. 365.
5. Altekar, *The Position of Women.*
6. I owe this reference to Professor Michael Witzel.
7. A. B. Keith, ed. and trans., *The Aitrareya āraṇyaka* (Oxford: Clarendon Press, 1909), pp. 121, 123.
8. Patrick Olivelle, *The Early Upaniṣads* (New York and Oxford: Oxford University Press, 1998), p. 580.
9. Robert Ernest Hume, The *Thirteen Principal Upanishads* (2nd ed., revised) (London: Oxford University Press, 1968), pp. 294–301.
10. S. Radhakrishnan, ed., *The Principal Upaniùads* (Atlantic Highlands, NJ: Humanities Press, 1972 [1953]), pp. 521–22.
11. Keith, *The Aitrareya āraṇyaka,* p. 121 note 1.

CHAPTER 12

1. Ian Brownlie, ed., *Basic Documents on Human Rights* (3rd ed.) (Oxford: Clarendon Press, 1992), pp. 182–83.
2. Brownlie, ed., *Basic Documents on Human Rights,* p. 184.
3. Brownlie, ed., *Basic Documents on Human Rights,* p. 184, emphasis added.
4. Based on the account provided by Vettam Mani, *Puràṇic Encyclopedia* (Delhi: Motilal Banarsidass, 1975), p. 873. The following ègVedic verse alludes to the liberation of śunaḥśepa (I.26.12–13):

   § 12. By night, by day they tell me, as tells me too
   This longing of my heart: "Whom śunaḥśepa
   Called upon, bound [and captive as he was],
   Varuṇa, the king, may he release (muc-) us!"

   § 13. For śunaḥśepa, captive, manacled
   To three stakes, called upon the son of Aditi,
   Varuõa, the king, that he might free him:
   May the wise one, undeceived, all fetters loose!

   [R. C. Zaehner, *Hindu Scriptures* (New York: Dutton, 1966), p. 4.]
5. Stella Kramrisch, *Manifestations of Shiva* (Philadelphia: Philadelphia Museum of Art, 1981), p. xviii.

CHAPTER 13

1. P. V. Kane History of *Dharmaśāstra,* vol. III (2nd ed.), p. 399.

CHAPTER 14

1. Michael Ignatieff, *The Rights Revolution* (Toronto: Canadian Broadcasting Corporation, 2000), p. 1.
2. Klaus K. Klostermaier, *A Survey of Hinduism* (2nd ed.) (Albany, NY: State University of New York Press, 1994), p. 343.

CHAPTER 15

1. Hari Prasad Shastri, trans., *The Ramayana of Valmiki* (London: Shanti Sadan, 1992 [1959]), pp. 326–27.
2. Michael Ignatieff, "Is the Human Rights Era Ending?," *The New York Times,* February 5, 2002, p. A 29.
3. Rajeev Srinivasan, "Sri Jeyendra Sarasvati," *India Abroad,* March 8, 2002, p. 20.
4. Alison Dundes Renteln, *International Human Rights: Universalism vs. Relativism* (Newbury Park, California: Sage Publications, 1990), p. 17.
5. *Ràmàyaõa* VI.109.25 (vulgate); VI.99.39 (critical text).
6. Bühler, *The Laws of Manu,* p. 315.
7. Vaman Shrivram Apte, *The Practical Sanskrit-English Dictionary* (Delhi: Motilal Banarsidass, 1965), p. 208.
8. A. L. Basham, *The Wonder That Was India* (New Delhi: Rupa & Co. 1999 [1954]), p. 126.
9. Basham, *The Wonder That Was India.*
10. Basham, *The Wonder That Was India,* p. 9.
11. J. W. McCrindle, *Ancient India as Described by Megasthenes and Arrian* (Calcutta: Chuckervertty, Chatterjee & Co. Ltd., 1960 [1876–1877]), pp. 21–32.
12 Hartmut Scharfe, *The State in Indian Tradition* (Leiden: E. J. Brill, 1989), p. 185.
13 G. Bühler, trans., *The Laws of Manu* (Delhi: Motilal Banarsidass, 1967 [1886]), pp. 230–31.
14. P. V. Kane, *History of Dharmaśāstra* (Poona: Bhandarkar Oriental Research Institute 1973), vol. III (2nd ed.) p. 209.
15. Basham, *The Wonder That Was India,* p. 126. Also see Scharfe, *The State in Indian Tradition,* p. 184.
16. Basham, *The Wonder That Was India,* p. 124.
17. Basham, *The Wonder That Was India,* p. 54, 126.
18. K. B. Panda, *Sanàtan Drama and Law* (Cuttack: Goswami Press, 1977), p. 69.
19. Bühler, *The Laws of Manu,* p. 230, emphasis added.
20. Basham, *The Wonder That Was India,* p. 123.
21. Percival Spear, ed., *The Oxford History of India by the Late Vincent A. Smith, C.J.E.* (4th ed.) (Delhi: Oxford University Press, 1994), p. 79.

CHAPTER 16

1. Radha Kumud Mookherji, "Foreign Invasions", in R. C. Majumdar, ed., *The Age of Imperial Unity* (Bombay: Bharatiya Vidya Bhavan, 1951), p. 53.
2. R. C. Majumdar, *The Classical Accounts of India* (Calcutta: Firma KLM Private Ltd., 1981), pp. 42–43.
3. *The Gazette,* Montreal, October 4, 1998, p. C6.
4. I owe this insight to Marie Royer.
5. John Witte, Jr., "Law, Religion, and Human Rights", *Columbia Human Rights Law Review,* vol. 28, no. 1 (Fall 1996), p. 13.
6. Gregory Baum, "Human Rights: An Ethical Perspective," *The Ecumenist* (May/June 1994), p. 65.
7. Sumner B. Twiss, "Moral Grounds and Plural Cultures: Interpreting Human Rights in the International Community," *Journal of Religious Ethics* 26.2 (Fall 1998), p. 272.
8. Ninian Smart and Shivesh Thakur, eds., *Ethical and Political Dilemmas of Modern India* (New York: St. Martin's Press, 1993), p. xi.
9. Louis Henkin, "Religion, Religions and Human Rights," *Journal of Religious Ethics* 26.2 (Fall 1981), p. 232.
10. Henkin, *"Religion, Religions and Human Rights."*
11. Henkin, *"Religion, Religions and Human Rights,"* p. 236, emphasis added.
12. Henkin, "Religion, Religions and Human Rights."
13. Henkin, "Religion, Religions and Human Rights."
14. Henkin, "Religion, Religions and Human Rights."
15. William Thorsell, "Whose Justice Is It?" *The Globe and Mail,* Toronto, January 9, 1999, p. D6.
16. Thorsell, "Whose Justice Is It?"

APPENDIX II

1. See Jeffrey Burton Russell, *Inventing the Flat Earth: Columbus and Modern Historians* (New York: Praeger, 1991), passim.
2. K. Satchidananda Murty, *Revelation and Reason in Advaita Vedànta* (New York: Columbia University Press, 1959), p. 312.
3. Christopher Chapple, *The Bhagavad Gītà: Translated by Winthrop Sargeant* (Albany, NY: State University of New York Press, 1984), p. 10.
4. Satischandra Chatterjee and Dhirendramohan Datta, *An Introduction to Indian Philosophy* (Calcutta: University of Calcutta, 1968), p. 9.
5. A. L. Basham, *The Wonder That Was India* (3rd ed. revised) (New Delhi: Rupa & Co., 1999), pp. 216–17.
6. Basham, *The Wonder That Was India,* p. 96.
7. Basham, *The Wonder That Was India,* p. 9. Also see p. 152.

8. Arvind Sharma, *Are Human Rights Western? A Contribution to the Dialogue of Civilizations* (New Delhi: Oxford University Press, 2006), passim.
9. Basham, *The Wonder That Was India,* p. 137.
10. Basham, *The Wonder That Was India,* p. 340.
11. Basham, *The Wonder That Was India,* p. 113.
12. Wilhelm Halbfass, *India and Europe: An Essay in Understanding* (Albany, NY: State University of New York Press, 1988).
13. Halbfass, *India and Europe,* pp. 330, 333, 554 n. 101.
14. Halbfass, *India and Europe,* p. 330.
15. Halbfass, *India and Europe,* p. 333.
16. P. V. Kane, *History of Dharmaśāstra* (Poona: Bhandarkar Oriental Research Institute, 1977), vol. V Pt. II (2nd ed,), p. 1637. The following extract also testifies to the wide diffusion of this category (Kane, p. 10–11): "Yàj (I.122) mentions nine qualities as the means of securing dharma for all (from the *bràhmaṇa* to the *cāṇḍālas*). The *Mahàbhàrata* says that freedom from anger, truthfulness, sharing one's wealth with others, forbearance, procreation (of children) from one's wife (alone), purity, absence of enmity, straightforwardness, maintaining persons dependent on oneself—these nine are the duties of all *varṇas.* The *Vàmanapuràṇa* says that tenfold dharma is common to all and names these ten as *ahiṁsà, satya, asteya, dàna,* forbearance, restraint, quiescence, not demeaning oneself, purity, tapas. Hemàdri (*vratakhaṇḍa* pp. 7–8) quotes several passages from the *Brahma, Brahmavaivarta,* and *Viùõudharmottara* for several *sàdhàraṇa dharmas* (virtues common to all *varṇas* and *àśramas*). The *Viṣṇudharmasūtra* enumerates fourteen qualities as *sàmànya-dharma.*"
17. Patrick Olivelle, *The Law Code of Manu* (New York: Oxford University Press, 2004), p. 184.
18. Olivelle, *The Law Code of Manu,* p. 105.
19. Kane, *History of Dharmaśāstra,* vol. II Part I, p. 11.
20. R. P. Kangle, *The Kauṭilīya Arthaśāstra* (Delhi: Motilal Banarsidass, 1969), Part I, p. 5.
21. Barbara Stoler Miller, *Yoga: Discipline of Freedom* (Berkeley: University of California Press, 1996), pp. 53–54.
22. Donald Eugene Smith, *India as a Secular State* (Princeton, NJ: Princeton University Press, 1963), p. 292ff.
23. Arvind Sharma, *Hindu Scriptural Value System and the Economic Development of India* (New Delhi: Heritage Publishers, 1980), pp. 66–67.
24. Julius Lipner, *Hindus: Their Religious Beliefs and Practices* (London and New York: Routledge, 1994), pp. 223–24.
25. Lipner, *Hindus,* p. 225.
26. Personal communication from Dr. Neelima Shukla-Bhatt, Department of Religion, Wellesley College, dated April 4, 2006.

Index

About the Author

Arvind Sharma has been a member of the Faculty of Religious Studies at McGill University since 1987. He has held fellowships at the Center for the Study of World Religions, the Center for the Study of Values in Public Life, and the Center for Business and Government, John F. Kennedy School of Government, at Harvard University; and at the Brookings Institute. He also received a Maxwell Fellowship and was elected Fellow of the Royal Asiatic Society, London in 1987. He is the author of *Are Human Rights Western?* (2006) and *Religious Studies and Comparative Methodology* (2005), and the editor of *Part of the Problem, Part of the Solution: Religion Today and Tomorrow* (2008) and *The World's Religions after September 11* (2008).